LIFE BEHIND THE MASK

by

Alden Edward

DORRANCE
PUBLISHING CO
EST. 1920
PITTSBURGH, PENNSYLVANIA 15238

Dorrance Publishing Co
585 Alpha Drive
Pittsburgh, PA 15238
Visit our website at *www.dorrancebookstore.com*

ISBN: 978-1-6491-3841-5
eISBN: 978-1-6491-3859-0

Dedications

This book is dedicated to those who have had an incredible impact on my life and growth as a person. I'll start off with my mom and dad, without whom I would not be here. Yes, chuckle warranted. But they both influenced me in different ways, some of compassion, some of discipline, some of understanding how people are different, and those differences should be respected. They are my rocks. My dad passed away fourteen years ago but is still here with me today. My mom is a spitfire, who I love to banter with. These people are the foundation of my writing structure.

I would also like to dedicate this endeavor to my amazing, loving, intelligent, and patient wife. She is sincerely the love of my life and provides me comfort, support, and is a great "comma" critic. Yes, I am comma-challenged. I am so happy to have written this book under a roof with her, under shelter at home orders. I will spend 24/7 with her for the rest of my life.

Jack and Jackie Heelan. Jackie has been my mother's best friend since high school. Jackie was there with my mom as my father was passing and greeted me as I went into the hospital room. She is a saint. Jack and Jackie were a part of my marriage to Donna and the marriage ceremony. Jack is an amazing financier, mentor, and friend.

Ronald Cappodano, my mentor and great friend. When I was in my twenties, he showed me what strength and family really is, beyond your biological relatives. He has touched so many lives, inclusive of my own, as has his wife Irene. I would not be here today without them. Ron and Irene, you are an amazing example of love and commitment that we should all strive to have.

There are so many more that I would like to acknowledge, but you will get bored with my effusive thanks and love for these individuals. Just know that all of my family and friends are a part of this story because they are the tapestry of my life, and because of their support and input from their own experiences, they have made me who I am today.

I Will Write

I will write
I will write with passion
From the heart
Don't tell me to describe, don't tell
I'll do what I want
This is my story

Place trust in yourself
Give into reality
Be your own, honest self
Love like there is no tomorrow
Honor your inner self

My passion is being truthful
Being myself
Loving my wife and family
Loving those around me
Being a unique individual
I will never stop being a unique individual

Take my hand and let's walk forward together
We can shout at the top of our lungs
I am me
I am good
And I am worthwhile

Don't discount me but instead count on me.

Life Behind the Mask

Chapter 1. It Arrived

It was like Neville Shute's novel *On the Beach*. Except for the fact that the invisible enemy was not nuclear fallout, it was a nefarious virus, COVID-19. We were experiencing World War III, in a manner that most people had never imagined. The outside world was eerily silent, with the infrequent exception of a car passing by or a dog barking. If you had to go to the grocery store, you were urged to wear a mask and social distance, keeping a six-foot perimeter around you, away from other people. Some stores even metered how many people could be in the store at any given time and taped arrows on the floor to direct traffic, such that people would not walk directly towards each other. Get what you need and then get out. That was the typical plan. Buy enough for two weeks, if you can. Nonperishables became a necessity, hand sanitizer, soap, paper towels, and toilet paper became worth their weight in gold.

This virus did not discriminate based on age, race, ethnicity, gender, social status, wealth, fame, political persuasion, or intelligence; this was an equal opportunity killer. Having said that, age, ethnicity, and economic status did have an impact with African-Americans, Latinos, Native Americans, the elderly, those with pre-existing conditions, and those of lower socioeconomic status bearing the brunt of the killer's force. The virus was being fair, but our societal structure was not equally so designed.

Misinformation was coming from the highest of places, and the only thing that could be hoped for was that politics could be taken out of the equation. But this was an election year, so what would be anticipated became the reality of the day. Primaries cancelled and no definitive end in sight. This had become an argument pitting the economy versus health and human safety, and in many but not all instances, Republicans versus Democrats and the President, well, against anyone who did not agree with everything that he had to say.

Shelter in place had become the norm, so phone and video chats replaced a lot of human interactions. Businesses suffered immensely, as did their employees who could not come to work, and in many instances, therefore, did not get paid. Restaurants closed their doors; the only options were takeout or delivery. Hair salons, barbershops, and nail parlors, closed. Peoples hair grew long and turned new colors. Nails broke off and hair extensions came out. Individuals in abusive relationships had to shelter in place with their abuser. People had to learn how to live in this "new normal." Some people handled it well and others, not so much.

People who could work from home had to come to grips with being around their family members 24/7, and those with preteen children needed to establish a balance between work and home schooling. High school students needed to learn to take their courses online, as did college students. Even a more difficult challenge for college students was the loss of the independence that they had previously gained. These were very hard times.

Chapter 2.
Solace in Sheltering from Home

I have become entranced by the motion of the trees, the leaves that are starting to grow and the birds outside my window, which look so at peace. It gives me solace. I guess that I have always been used to moving at the speed of sound, I can't claim light… I am not that fast. But this was a time to take a deep breath; quite ironic in the context of the COVID-19 pandemic. One can find simple things to keep them amused at times like these. My wife and I named the two squirrels that are always in our back yard, and my wife explained to me that Pumpkin was the one with white under his tail and Muffin's tail was 100% grey. What a relief that was.

View out of my office window

There was something scary but magical about this time. I know that sounds odd, but it just made different parts of my brain spring to life. People all over were connecting from a safe distance. We were talking and possibly more engaged than ever. Humanity was rising to the challenge, at least most of it. I will get to that in a bit. Essential workers were extremely grateful when you acknowledged them. People were showing immense gratitude towards those on the front line. In some places, people would stream onto their porches or balconies and applaud or bang pots for the essential workers as they came home. Signs with the words "Thank You" were placed in people's windows. Random acts of kindness were also occurring. Individuals were taking the time to care for their neighbors with underlying conditions and the elderly, buying them groceries, so that they did not need to put themselves at risk going out in public.

Sheltering at home actually felt like freedom versus being outside or at a place providing essential services behind the mask. The mask was isolating, suffocating, and generally uncomfortable but necessary. People had hoarded the most effective masks that health care providers desperately needed, and that created a lot of angst. My wife and I had one mask that I kept in the garage. It was one that remained from those we had purchased some time ago when we were conducting mold remediation in our basement.

When it was my first time to go to the store after face covering was part of the guidelines, I went out to the garage to get it. I pulled it off of the shelf, and as it got down to eye level, I saw one letter and two numbers printed boldly on the side, N95. I recoiled slightly. Not that this was a bad thing for me because these are very effective, in fact these are the masks that those on the frontline needed the most. I went into the house and told my wife that I was getting ready to go to the store and that I hoped I would not get beaten up. She laughed and said why? I showed her the mask, and she gasped. She said you can't go out with this.

"I'll be fine," I said. "I was just shocked when I saw what it was."
"Give it to me!" she said and promptly grabbed a black sharpie that happened to be handy and colored out the N95 on the mask.

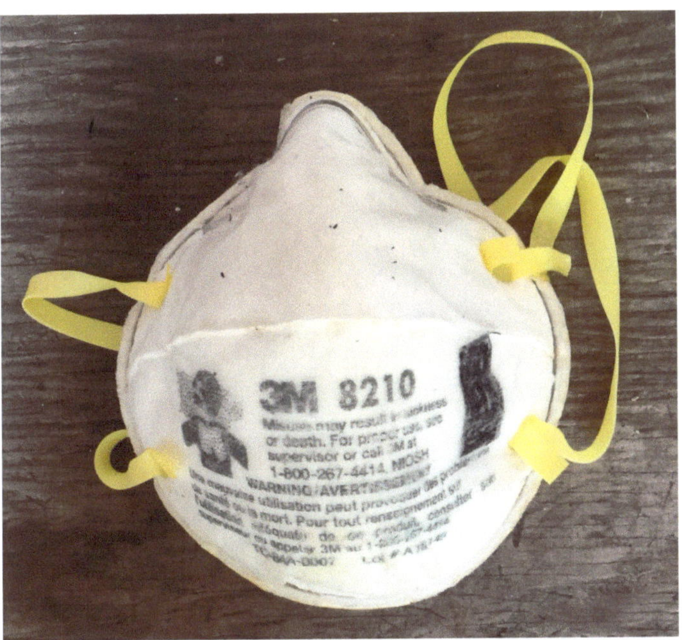

The original mask. Notice the blacked-out rectangle on the right. Yes, it has seen better days. Funny, I never saw it before, but it cautions that "Misuse may result in sickness or death." Ironic, huh?

Eventually that mask became my best friend outside of the house. I have finally learned how to breath effectively wearing it. People are being very creative, I have seen men wearing washcloth masks, hand towel masks, ski masks, and even a very creatively crafted pink and blue paisley mask. That gentleman was not at all happy with it, and when I commented on it, he blamed it on his significant other. One can still find humor in this time of general fear, discomfort, and despair.

I have randomly asked people when I am out and about how do you feel about wearing "the mask," and the typical response is, "It's hot but necessary," or "It makes it a bit hard to breath." Therein is the crux of this experience.

The weather finally started getting better, and it was possible to be outside while following the social distancing guidelines. In fact during this time, I found an additional use for my mask, protecting my lungs from the Turf Builder,® Weed & Feed that I needed to lay down on the lawn. That stuff is toxic. I know that you are not supposed to re-wear the masks, but you could not get one anywhere. Even if you were able to find them online, they often were not being shipped for quite some time. I wore that trusty old N95 until the bands snapped. I had to superglue the mask together temporarily, but luckily masks that I had ordered one and a half months prior arrived the following week, and friends and family sent along homemade masks as well. My original N95 is officially retired, but I can't bring myself to throw it out. It has been in quarantine for three weeks now, so I don't think that it poses any threat to the shelf on which it resides, and it is socially distanced from all of the tools.

Masks are a funny thing. They can be and are becoming fashion statements. I now have more masks than I probably need. Some personalized with images, some black, some white, and some blue. If this becomes part of our new normal, I think that there is a booming industry out there to make these masks as visually appealing as possible.

Chapter 3.
The Best and the Worst in People

The best and the worst in people was realized. Those on the front lines risked their lives every day. Personal protective equipment (PPE) was constantly in short supply, but doctors, nurses, EMTs, police, and fire fighters put themselves at risk every day due to the commitment they had to their professions. Essential workers, such as those in the grocery stores, postal workers, and other delivery service personnel needed to do their jobs. Individuals involved in food delivery established a new way to function, I call it the "Drop, Ring, and Run."

Although I mentioned that the virus does not discriminate, our government does. Protect the White House at any cost. Testing every day. Make sure that the President does not need to wear a mask. But testing and PPE for the broader population is not quite equally available. In fact those working to save lives (doctors, nurses, EMTs, pharmacists, policemen, and firemen), putting themselves at risk of contracting COVID-19 have experienced shortages of PPE and supplies needed for testing, such as swabs and reagents. These people have been contracting the virus and dying. As of early April, nearly 10,000 healthcare professionals had contracted the virus and twenty-seven had died. These numbers are likely an underestimate and will just keep going up, as some institutions are not collecting this data systematically (https://www.usnews.com/news/national-news/articles/2020-04-14/cdc-nearly-10-000-health-care-workers-had-covid-19).

Additionally Federal workers were also experiencing increased numbers of cases (https://www.govexec.com/workforce/2020/04/more-10000-federal-employees-have-contracted-covid-19/164986/).

APRIL 28, 2020

Defense Department: As of Tuesday afternoon, the Pentagon had confirmed 1,091 cases among civilian workers. An additional 4,265 military personnel tested positive, as well as 427 contractors.

Veterans Affairs Department: VA has confirmed 1,633 cases among its Veterans Health Administration employees. VA employees have expressed significant concern about the lack of personal protective equipment, policies that threaten discipline or loss of pay if they do not come in after exposure and poor communication from management. Twenty VA employees have died from symptoms related to the virus.

U.S. Postal Service: USPS has confirmed 1,606 employees tested positive for the virus in its workforce of 630,000. The Postal Service has sought to make gloves and masks available in all of its workstations after employees for weeks said basic items were not available. Cases among postal workers jumped by 33% in the last week.

State Department: State has confirmed 436 cases in its workforce, most of which are currently active. More than 2,800 employees are self-isolating due to possible exposure. Five State Department employees have died from symptoms related to the virus.

Transportation Security Administration: TSA has seen 495 employees test positive for COVID-19. All told about 1,000 Homeland Security Department workers have tested positive, according to a *Buzzfeed* report. At least seventeen Federal Emergency Management Agency workers have contracted the virus.

Agriculture Department: At USDA's Food Safety Inspection Service, at least 100 employees have tested positive. The agency is struggling to keep employees safe as hotspots have developed at meat processing plants around the country.

Internal Revenue Service: 100 IRS employees have contracted the coronavirus. The agency asked 10,000 workers to return to their offices this week.

Health and Human Services Department: HHS has spearheaded and coordinated much of the federal response, and so far seventy-four employees have tested positive for the virus.

Interior Department: At least ten National Park Service employees have tested positive. NPS made all parks free during the pandemic, though a growing number have since closed. Interior also declined to provide updated figures across its bureaus.

Chapter 4. A Shift in Our Culture

The number of influential individuals who contracted this scourge and passed away changed the entire landscape of politics, the media, entertainment, the arts, sports, and so much more. We lost icons who championed women's right to vote, who stood up for human rights and civil rights, who battled segregation, who worked on the Manhattan project, Patriots who served in WWII, the Vietnam war, the Korean war, and the Iraq war. We lost mothers, fathers, grandparents, children, aunts, uncles and young adults who could have significantly contributed to society, to their families, and their communities. We lost talented musicians, scientists, actors, Broadway stars, magicians, teachers, first responders, icons… I hate to say it, but some would comment that a number of these individuals were just old. That does not mean that they had to die. What in the heck does that have to do with anything? Being old is just a situation in the chronology of life. No one has a sand glass that says this is your time. It does not matter how old you are, but we have lost a lot of our history with this virus, and that should weigh heavy on all of our minds.

Interestingly as of July 9th, 2020, over 130,000 Americans have died due to COVID-19, which eerily echoes the 100,000+ individuals killed by the atomic bombs (code named "little boy" and "fat man") in Hiroshima and Nagasaki, Japan. So this IS really WWIII. Are we now at a point in time where we can only say goodbye to our loved ones via phone or online?

Chapter 5.
I Am Not Taking My Mask Off

They started lifting the shelter in place guidelines and began to reopen the economy. Not because it was the right thing to do but because our President could not stand to see what the safety precautions were doing to the economy, and the President's followers started becoming enraged. The President absolutely refused to wear a mask in public, and as a result, so did many but not all of his followers.

People were heard to say, "If the President of the United States is not wearing one, then neither am I." It was described as a loss of personal freedom. Personal freedom to what, infect someone if you are an asymptomatic carrier? Hey, look, the herd immunity approach did not work that well for Sweden.

I personally am not taking my mask off in the near future, not just for me but the health of others. I walk in the grocery store, go to the gas station, or to the hardware store with my mask on and abide the social distancing guidelines. I bite my tongue every time someone approaches me without a mask and is not social distancing. Would I like to say something, absolutely, but they clearly already don't care about my health and well-being, so if I were to say something, who knows what would ensue. Do I want to get back to normal, yes, but I am not going to ignore the fact that times change, things change, and as a species, we need to adapt. It may be a "new normal," but that does not mean it has to be a bad thing.

Businesses have become savvy to where we are today. No one wants to wear a black, white, or blue mask all the time when they are out in public. Companies have taken to making custom masks with any image that you chose (I am certain that there are some limitations). Will custom masks become the newest fashion trend? I don't know, but stranger things have happened.

Chapter 6. Breathe!

Breathe has taken on an even more impactful meaning beyond COVID-19. I don't think that anyone has not heard of George Floyd at this point, but he was a forty-six-year-old father of two, and he died at the hands of police in Minneapolis, Minnesota on May 25th, 2020. He was sought out after a store clerk called police to indicate that he thought that Floyd had given him a counterfeit $20 bill. Derek Chauvin, a white officer, pressed his knee to Floyd's neck for almost nine minutes while Floyd was handcuffed face down on the ground. Three additional officers were also involved in the restraint of Floyd and prevented onlookers from intervening. A young woman and other onlookers had the wherewithal to capture the events on video. During the last three minutes, Floyd was motionless with no pulse. An ambulance was called to the scene. George Floyd had gone into cardiac arrest and was pronounced dead at a nearby hospital. In his last minutes, he cried out for his mama, who had passed away years earlier. Where there is no justice, there is truly no peace.

He is not the first, nor sadly, he will likely not be the last. The statement "I can't breathe" will forever be in our memories. These were the last words of Eric Garner as well, July 17th, 2014. Now for more reasons than COVID-19, these words need to be understood by the American people. This is a pandemic-x2. At this point, we are working our way into extinction. If the virus and our unwillingness to comply with expert guidance doesn't do it, then we will take care of it ourselves, one innocent life at a time. Our lives are being shattered by a "false god." All of humanity deserves more than this.

We are now well over 135,000 deaths as of July 9th, 2020, and with the protests occurring now due to the George Floyd murder and the President's insistence on having large gatherings indoors, that number is likely to go up. These protests are important to counter a significant injustice and a need for reform in policing, but this is just compounding the impact of COVID-19. These massive rally gatherings only benefit one person.

"I can't breathe," George Floyd said. "I CAN'T BREATHE!" How can someone in the role of protecting our citizens not understand what that means? "I CAN'T BREATHE!" My thought is wake up! No, not George because he can't! However, we as a nation need to wake up! There are too many instances of unnecessary violence from police and lay citizens. What has pushed our country in this direction? I have my opinions, but what are yours? Do the words "I CAN'T BREATHE" mean anything to you? I doubt you would like to hear those words uttered from any of your family or friends. Come on, this is personal… None of us probably have known George Floyd or many of the others who have uttered those same words, but that does not make the state of the union ok.

"I CAN'T BREATHE!" Take it in…pun absolutely intended. Can we all collectively take a moment and hold our breath for eight minutes and forty-nine seconds? Guess that in trying none of us would get to the end of this book or essentially the end of the day. I personally tried and could not get past two minutes. "I CAN'T BREATHE!" We are all human beings, and this American flag was created for every American, not just a few.

"Strange fruit" is a very emotional song. Billie Holiday had it right. The emotion on her face when she sang this told it all. Currently it does not refer to lynching on the trees but on the ground. This is unfortunately not a new type of story being covered by the media. See below a report in Rolling Stone magazine from 2014. We have clearly not come as far forward as we thought.

Faces of Injustice. The toll is not inconsequential. There is a name, a family and a story behind each of these individuals.

A report from 2014 on people of color killed by the police
https://www.rollingstone.com/politics/politics-news/black-lives-matter-11-racist-police-killings-with-no-justice-served-40001/

1. Amadou Diallo (1999)

Four NYPD officers notoriously rained forty-one bullets down onto Diallo in the Bronx, killing the unarmed Guinean immigrant as he tried to enter his apartment building. They later claimed to have seen Diallo reaching for something that looked like a weapon; in fact all he had in his hand was a wallet. The incident sparked national headlines and civil rights marches, as well as Bruce Springsteen's protest song **"American Skin (41 Shots)"** – but all four police officers were acquitted of all charges in the case. One of the killer cops, Kenneth Boss, remained on the force **and was allowed to carry an NYPD gun again** in 2012.

2. Patrick Dorismond (2000)

Dorismond was hanging out in Manhattan with a friend when an undercover cop approached and asked where he could score some weed – blatant profiling based on Dorismond's appearance. A confrontation ensued, and another officer shot him fatally in the chest. Then–Mayor Rudy Giuliani released the twenty-six-year-old security guard's sealed juvenile legal records in an effort to smear his police force's latest victim, infamously saying that the dead man was no "altar boy;" it was later revealed that Dorismond had attended the same Catholic school as the mayor and served as an altar boy in his youth. A grand jury chose not to indict the officer who shot Dorismond to death.

3. Ousmane Zongo (2003)

The NYPD crossed paths with Zongo at a storage facility in Manhattan during a raid on a counterfeit CD ring. Zongo, an unarmed forty-three-year-old immigrant from Burkina Faso who repaired art had nothing to do with the raid, but police shot him four times when they saw him in a corridor. The officer who killed Zongo was convicted of criminally negligent homicide – but a judge sentenced him to no more than five years of probation and 500 hours of community service for taking an innocent man's life.

4. Timothy Stansbury (2004)

NYPD Officer Richard Neri fatally shot Stansbury, an unarmed nineteen-year-old, during a late-night patrol of a Bedford-Stuyvesant housing project. Neri said it was an accident, and a grand jury believed him, declining to return an indictment. The only punishment he faced was a thirty-day suspension from the force. Neri was later elected to a prestigious position in a New York police union.

5. Sean Bell (2006)

The night before his wedding, Bell and some friends went to a strip club in Queens for his bachelor party. When they left the club around 4:15 A.M. the next morning – Bell's wedding day – they ran afoul of a group of undercover and plainclothes NYPD cops, who fired an astonishing fifty bullets into the twenty-three-year-old's car, killing him instantly. The case led to major protests, but all three police officers charged in the case were acquitted.

6. Oscar Grant (2009)

On New Year's Day 2009, Bay Area transit officer Johannes Mehserle detained Grant on a subway platform after reports of a fight. The unarmed twenty-two-year-old was lying face-down on the ground when Mehserle shot and killed him, as captured on video by many bystanders. Mehserle was charged with murder, but the jury convicted him of a lesser crime, and he ended up serving less than a year for killing Grant.

7. Aiyana Stanley-Jones (2010)

Aiyana Stanley-Jones was just seven-years-old when a Detroit SWAT team took her life. Late at night, searching for a suspect in her neighborhood, the police threw a flash grenade through her family's window, stormed the house, and shot the little girl in her sleep. The raid occurred while the SWAT team was accompanied by a camera crew from the reality show *The First 48*. There have been two trials so far, both ending in mistrials.

8. Ramarley Graham (2012)

Plainclothes narcotics cops chased eighteen-year-old Graham into his family's home in the Bronx for unclear reasons. They shot and killed him at the door of his family's bathroom. A tiny quantity of marijuana was later found in the toilet, hardly enough to justify an instant death sentence for a teenager. The cop who killed Graham was not indicted, but a federal investigation is ongoing.

9. Tamon Robinson (2012)

An NYPD patrol car collided with Robinson at a Brooklyn housing project, killing him, after responding to a report that Robinson was digging up paving stones to sell them for some extra cash. He was unarmed. A police report claimed that Robinson caused his own fatal injuries by running into a stationary patrol car, but eyewitnesses said the cops rammed their vehicle into the twenty-seven-year-old; a few months later, the department had the gall to try and bill Robinson's grieving family for $710 for damage to the car. Two years later, the case has yet to go before a grand jury.

10. Rekia Boyd (2012)

Off-duty Chicago cop Dante Servin opened fire from his car into a group of people on the street, claiming he perceived a threat to his life. Twenty-two-year-old Rekia Boyd was among the people on the scene;

she died after taking a bullet to the head. Servin has been indicted (making him the first Chicago police officer in many years to face trial for a fatal shooting), but his case was recently delayed to 2015.

11. Kimani Gray (2013)
Plainclothes NYPD officers confronted the sixteen-year-old Gray in Brooklyn. Police claimed that he pulled a gun before they shot him to death on the street, but Gray's family disputed this allegation. Prosecutors announced this summer that they are not pursuing charges against the officers who killed the teenager.

Chapter 7. Plausible Deniability

"Plausible deniability is the ability of an individual, generally one of high rank or position, to deny that they had information about activities committed by others in a business, organization, or government, which led to abuse or illegal actions."

"The goal of plausible deniability is to allow a person to shift the blame onto other participants who were involved in the potentially illegal or immoral actions. Plausible deniability often allows a party, which may actually be partly responsible for the actions, to insulate themselves from any legal or civil penalties."

The President uses this all of the time when something happens related to the White House.

"Sorry, I don't know him/her, can you get me their name and I will follow up."

"No, I wasn't involved in that, but I will look into it."
"I don't know, why don't you ask China?"
"I can't hear you (through that mask)."

"That was just a nasty question." And I could go on. I am not saying anything that is not documented on video or in writing. This is a short chapter but accurate just the same.

I actually think that this is a "beautiful" chapter, absolutely beautiful. So beautiful. You could not make it any more beautiful.

Chapter 8.
A Game Theory Evaluation of the Response to the Pandemic

So could we have predicted that this was the way that the response to the pandemic would transpire? The answer is a resounding YES! Game theory would describe this as a competitive, asymmetrical game with rules that can be manipulated and many players, with their own unique perspectives and intentions. The fact that this is an election year means that the President could not ignore his staunch supporters and therefore do what is right. He needed to say what they wanted to hear, even if it wasn't true. He scoffed in the face of the US population by refusing to wear a mask, not a really good example for the country. He blamed China for what happened in the US, yet he was late to respond to the first cases. One model predicted that if he had acted even one week earlier, it could have saved >36,000 lives, according to research conducted by Columbia University and reported on May 21st, 2020.

On the flip side, those who disagreed with The President's approach to the pandemic listened to the expert clinicians who were outlining best practice and providing realistic approaches to decreasing the number of cases, focusing on a safe interaction with society. They had a belief in science and medicine, however, they knew that by wearing masks themselves, they were protecting others, and to a certain degree, themselves. Droplets carrying the virus in the air could remain for up to eight minutes, and over time they became smaller and smaller, so they could penetrate a mask.

On the other hand, many of The President's supporters were in complete denial and many disregarded state guidance on social distancing and wearing masks. They took guns to protest at state capitals about stay at home rules and the closure of businesses, and some wore swastikas, showed images of lynching, harassed Asian-Americans, and verbally assaulted individuals in retail stores once they were able to reopen. However, there were some of the President's supporters who did mostly socially distance and wore masks. These were those who respected the broader community and themselves.

Interestingly some of The President's supporters referred to themselves as the red states and other states as the Commie blue states. This was an interesting assertion as both Russia and China are Communist states, and The President has provided leaders of both countries with accolades. He has soured on China a bit recently, but that may be based on what he thinks works best in this election year. The question for the everyday American became, who should I listen to? What does this mean for my future, socially, employment/income, my children's schooling, the health and well-being of my family, impact on my 401K? These questions are not so easy to answer without a clear strategy for moving forward.

So from a game theory perspective, we need to evaluate what the best outcome is for all individuals involved, knowing that people's individual decisions are not going to be communicated overtly. How to do that? Tap into their emotive drivers. Those are the thoughts and beliefs that are not overtly articulated.

Key points:

- The President is focused on his re-election and public image
- He has built a platform based on the economy
- He has a distain for people who disagree with or question him
- He thrives on conflict
- He is a pathologic liar, and when people contradict him and speak the truth, he calls it fake news or a political hit job
- He is vane
- He love-hates the media
- He has a "GOD" complex
- He denies responsibility for anything and believes that he is above the law
- He acts like a school child and calls anybody who he feels threatened by silly, degrading names
- He is a narcissist
- He does not believe in the biblical saying, "Do unto others as you would have them do unto you" as spoken by Jesus in Luke 6:31 and Matthew 7:12, which is commonly referred to as the "Golden Rule"
- Oh, and he loves golf

The President's supporters follow him blindly:

- If the President says it's true, well then, damnit, it's TRUE
- For the most part, they only listen to what they want to hear
- Many of them hate the media, unless it substantiates their beliefs
- **They believe:**
    - That Trump is a devote Christian
    - The economy is improving because of him
    - "Millions voted illegally" and that is why he lost the popular vote in 2016

- Immigration is out of control and illegal immigrants are all violent criminals
- The President should have the power to overturn judicial rulings
- His plans for healthcare are beautiful, and President Obama's healthcare legislation is an absolute failure
- Barack Obama was not born in the United States and he is a Muslim
- There's a war on gun owners
- All the investigations into the President's ties to Russia are bogus
- The President should not have been impeached by the Congress
- The President is honest and trustworthy
- They don't believe in the first amendment, as it relates to the freedom of the press, but they do believe in it as it relates to freedom of speech/expression, and assembly
- They believe in the second amendment regarding the right to bear arms
- They believe in the ninth amendment that protects rights not enumerated in the constitution (let's all try to figure out what this means)
- Not all, but many, don't believe in the fifteenth amendment that prohibits the denial of the right to vote based on race, color, or previous condition of servitude
- **Psychological traits of The President's supporters** (T.F. Pettigrew, Journal of Social and Political Psychology 2017, Vol. 5(1), 107–116).
    - Authoritarian Personality Syndrome
    - Social dominance orientation
    - Prejudice
    - Intergroup contact
    - Relative deprivation

**Republicans who are not supporters of
the President:**

- Are less racially motivated in their beliefs

- Are independent thinkers and utilize facts to
  make determinations regarding what is best for
  both themselves and others

- More often than not, do not experience
  relative deprivation

- Retain historic Republican values and do not
  follow blindly

- Can see through the President's lies and
  understand the implications

- Are focused on retaining a Republican Senate
  and winning the House

Democrats/Independents for the President:

- The economy has taken its toll on their lives
  and they are willing to throw up a "hail Mary"
  and see if the President really can bring the
  economy back

- More often than not, are white

- Are more likely to describe themselves as an
  independent

**Democrats/Independents who are not
supporting the President:**

- Need a change from this dysfunctional
  administration

- Feel that if the President is elected to four
  more years, it could take us down a slippery
  slope and unravel our democracy, as it was
  originally designed

- Believe that chaos will likely ensue when the
  President becomes a "lame duck" President and
  feel that it is better that happens now rather
  than in 2024

- Understand that taking safety precautions
  during this pandemic not only protects them
  but also those around them

- See the bigotry in his statements
- Have respect for others
- Just want to be out of this chaos that has consumed our country for four years

Ok, so let's look at the best payoff for the President. He needs to win the 2020 Presidential election. All of the other things that he sees as strategies either support this or are distractions, which is his go to strategy if the press reports on him unfavorably. For the President's supporters, the payoff is a continuation of the right to ignore social mores and have their personal and political interests satisfied. Mostly but not always, their only consideration is for themselves. The payoff for Republican, non-President supporters is to find a reasonable stance for the election of a congress and senate that can uphold the majority in the Senate and win the majority in the House to retain control of legislature. The payoff for non-Republican, non-President supporters is the election of a new President, with values and policy ideas that are more in-line with their way of thinking.

So what does all of this have to do with the pandemic? A lot actually. The President's mismanagement of the pandemic and exerting power to disperse peaceful protesters who were on the streets as a result of George Floyd's murder just pushes our country further into the weeds. No compassion. No real consideration of the repercussions of massive numbers of people gathering (although for good reason) without social distancing. This is where people put humanity before self. But the President felt the need to disperse the protesters in order to get a photo op in front of St. John's Episcopal Church holding a bible. Not praying or reading from it, just holding it. This is the only time that I will come close to mentioning his name in this book, but this is the ultimate example of Trumpian Psychopathology. We should probably add this to the Diagnostic and Statistical Manual of Mental Disorders, 5th edition (DSM-5).

A. The President and his supporters

B. The Democrats

	 1. Focus on what's best for the country	 2. Minimize importance of the pandemic	 3. Win at any cost
 1. Focus on what's best for the country	A=3 B=3 Net = 0 This is equilibrium	A=1 B=3 B nets 2	A=3 B=5 B nets 2
 2. Politicize the pandemic	A= 3 B=1 A nets 2	A= 2 B=3 B nets 1	A= 2 B=3 B nets 1
 3. Run a negative campaign*	A= 3 B=1 A nets 2	A=1 B= 2 B nets 1	A=3 B=2 A nets 1

* focusing on the President's lies and deceptions

Note: This is a simplified analysis for illustrative purposes. It involves two "players" and in this example includes three potential strategies for each. The importance of this simplified strategic analysis is the identification of an equilibrium strategy. At equilibrium neither group gets their maximum payoff, but the outcome nets a zero in terms of the payoff to each. Since there are 9 potential outcomes, we can apply numbers to analyze the payoff of each strategy taken by each group in comparison to the strategy taken by the other. This particular analysis focuses on the impact of the strategy taken by each player on Republican, Democrat and Independent voters with the primary objective being winning the election. Independent voters represent approximately 34% of the U.S. electorate, while Democrats and Republicans represent 33% and 29%, respectively. The direction of the scales indicates the potential directional impact of each strategy, i.e., right leaning, left leaning or balanced.

We can all see how this game nets out. There is really no full-on winner but moderation and compromise places every player on equal footing. It is a gambled chance, but nets all involved a chance of succeeding. What that means overall, we will know in a few months. Bottom line, in the current situation, no one is likely to be 100% happy, compliant, focused on the greater good, socially responsible, respectful, acknowledge what the implications of their actions are on them and those around them… I can go on, but if we don't take responsibility for our actions, then a net gain exercise is not possible. We need to take responsibility, being part of a diverse and "united" country. What we are seeing now are not American values.

So now let's see how the President fairs with the ten commandments, being the devote Christian that his followers believe he is. I'm just waiting forhim to hand out some purple coolaid.

<table>
<tr><td>

__The Ten Commandments (Exodus 20:2-17 NKJV) as rewritten by the President__

__1__"I am the Lord your God, who brought you out of the land of Egypt, out of the house of bondage. You shall have no other gods before Me. (this one pretty much stands but without the part about Egypt. I am not a fan of immigrants)

__2__"You shall not make for yourself a carved image, or any likeness of anything thatis in heaven above, or that is in the earth beneath, or that is in the water under the earth; you shall not bow down to them nor serve them. For I, the Lord your God, am a jealous God, visiting the iniquity of the fathers on the children to the third and fourth generations of those who hate Me, but showing mercy to thousands, to those who love Me and keep My Commandments.

</td></tr>
</table>

(Why carve in wood when you can chisel marble. I am "God," you know, so chisel any effigy of me but do not chisel any likeness of Barrack, Hillary, Michelle, Joe, Nancy, or any other democrat, despite the fact that I used to be one.)

3 *"You shall not take the name of the Lord your God in vain, for the Lord will not hold him guiltless who takes His name in vain* (unless you want to get fired from the administration or get a really negative post from me on Twitter).

4 *"Remember the Sabbath day, to keep it holy. Six days you shall labor and do all your work, but the seventh day is the Sabbath of the Lord your God. In it you shall do no work: you, nor your son, nor your daughter, nor your male servant, nor your female servant, nor your cattle, nor your stranger who is within your gates. For in six days the Lord made the heavens and the earth, the sea, and all that is in them and rested the seventh day. Therefore, the Lord blessed the Sabbath day and hallowed it* (because that is one of my golf days").

5 *"Honor your father and your mother, that your days may be long upon the land which the Lord your God is giving you* (mine are no longer with us, so we can scrap this one).

6 *"You shall not murder* (but you can do it in my name if it involves someone that I don't agree with, don't like, or generally feel that they will hurt my campaign).

7 *You shall not commit adultery* (Wait, I think that there's a typo in this one).

8 *"You shall not steal* (unless it is from people who enrolled in my university, worked on one of my many projects that went bankrupt, oh, or you are talking about stealing someone's dignity, yeah, do that whenever you want).

9 *"You shall not bear false witness against your neighbor* (I can, though. That is a given. You should probably follow this one, except if your neighbor has negative things to say about me, or has indicated that they won't vote for me in 2020, or you just don't like them based on race, gender, religious beliefs, socioeconomic status, or they are part of the LGBTQ community, are a Democrat, are an undocumented immigrant, think that I am fat, are glad that I was impeached by the House of Representatives, and think that the Senate chickened out, or they want gun control).

10 *"You shall not covet your neighbor's house; you shall not covet your neighbor's wife, nor his male servant, nor his female servant, nor his ox, nor his donkey, nor anything that is your neighbor's"* (Oh, heck, covet away. I do it all the time. I covet any dictators' powers. I covet any good-looking woman who passes my way. I covet fast food, especially hamburgers. I secretly covet Nancy Pelosi, as she is one strong mama. I covet Barrack's good looks and popularity. I covet the power of the military. I covet the word "beautiful." I covet the attention of the media, despite the fact that I constantly criticize them. I covet attention, period. I covet black sharpies. I covet what slave owners had before the civil war. I covet the reputation of Abe Lincoln because he was a Republican and very tall, slim, and damnit people love him. But I do not covet the abolition of slavery. How do you think I became a billionaire? What was he thinking?. I could go on, but this is probably enough to give you a taste of the value of coveting).

So based on game theory, what will the net be? It really all depends, not on the President but the American people and the rest of the world. "Act locally, think globally" comes to mind. If this chaos that has been created by this Commander and Chief, becomes a lasting new reality, what will this mean for us as a society? This is a country of the people, by the people and for the people. There are three branches of government for a reason. Did our current President get elected because he was legislatively knowledgeable? No. He got elected because people wanted a change from the bipartisan politics that had been at play. Guess what, he did nothing to "drain the swamp." All he did was play into the equation. He is no better than anyone he has called names in the past. In fact I would say that he is worse. I leave that to you to decide. My opinion only matters to me really, but I believe that we are all not so different that we can't see a positive path forward.

Chapter 9. Schadenfreude

Schadenfreude, "The pleasure derived from another person's misfortune." This applies to much of what we have been experiencing now. I go back once again to emotive drivers. Why do you act as you act, think what you think, believe what you believe? That third one is the trickiest since people may act on what they believe only because what they think may be most beneficial to them, not because it is the right thing to do in general. Belief is a funny thing. Most often it is brought up in the context of religion, and rightfully so. But belief is much deeper than that. What did we learn from our parents, broader family, friends, religious affiliations, teachers, colleagues, bosses? Religion and spirituality should not be divisive. These are very personal things. Race, skin color, gender, sexual orientation, political party, none of these things should be divisive. America was established as a melting pot. This is who we are, and this is what this virus is showing us. Come together, do not separate, except for from a six-foot distance until further notice. That is not how humanity can be recognized and humankind can be saved. Sorry, I will get off of my soapbox now. One final thought here…we are all human, so why can't we think about each other in that manner. I leave this up to "all y'all."

Chapter 10.
What Will Our New Normal Look Like?

Well, if we cannot unite around a single America, it may very well be extremely segmented. It is almost as if a new civil war is brewing. One where rational thinking is out the door and people rebel against those that they have historically put their trust in. Hopefully we haven't let ALL of the crazies out of the barn. Hey, look, I am not irrational. I am just a responsible American citizen who wants the best for our country. Yes, I believe that I am a Patriot in that way, not a Patriot in the manner that it has been redefined. Somehow we need to establish a new normal where we can all live together peacefully and focus on the well-being of the country as a whole. I know that is a big ask.

Much of this will be contingent upon the upcoming Presidential election. Can we somehow go back to being respectful of those around us, even if we were never completely there? Can we establish some level of civility and recognize, as the Declaration of Independence says, that all men (and women) are created equal?

So what is the new normal? It is not going to be the scenario described above. The nation needs to heal, which will take a long time and that will not occur under the current President. If our President is re-elected in 2020, we may face many more years of divisiveness, which at some point may become not the American Dream but our worst nightmare, making it very difficult to find a middle ground. I am not a Democrat or a Republican, I am an Independent and would vote for someone from either party, or even another party, such as the Vermont Progressive Party, the Independence Party of New York, or the Libertarian Party, which are all recognized by Congress, if their values and policy ideas seem as if they would be in the best interest of the American people and our global allies.

So the new normal? Well, it likely will be very new, similar to what we experienced post-9/11. I think that the first question that we need to answer is what is normal. Is it where we as individuals feel comfortable? Do we believe that normal is our experiences as we have grown up? Do we want normal to be what we want it to be? Are we so self-consumed that we can't look beyond the boundaries of our upbringing? We as a society need to do better. Life should not be like this. We should never emulate those who have no respect for humankind. Life is precious, and whether it is taken by a virus, a gun, or a knee to the neck, life must be respected. That is a right that we have as human beings… ALIVE. Just let that set in a bit. I ask that we all take a deep breath and ask the question, do I deserve to be alive? Do you? I believe that we all do, and no one should be unaccountable if they take that away from any of us. We are not God, the President is not God, and I would close with saying that we all need to respect our neighbors, our families, our friends, and honestly ourselves. We are not above God. We are not above the law. We are only as good as we act. Treat people as you would want to be treated yourself. Listen to this Mr. President, and by the way, try reading that book that you held high! Amen.

APPENDIX – National Impact of COVID-19

It is almost impossible to think about how the COVID-19 is shaping our US and global societies. The following excerpt from the New York Times, reproduced with permission, provides some perspective for the United States. This information is included to illustrate the human toll that the numbers represent. It includes a list of 1,000 individuals who died from COVID-19 with brief descriptions of who they were. Tellingly despite the fact that the list is long, it only represents <1% of the individuals lost to COVID-19 to date (May 27th, 2020).

I suggest that we all read through all of these names and contemplate the human, financial, cultural, mental and emotional health, social, political, and national security prices that we have paid, due to this virus and our nation's response to the pandemic.

America just passed a grim milestone in the coronavirus outbreak —
each figure here represents one of the nearly 100,043 lives lost so far
(as of May 27th, 2020). But a count reveals only so much. Memories,
gathered from obituaries across the country, help us to reckon with
what was lost.

THE NEW YORK TIMES, MAY 24TH, 2020

U.S. DEATHS NEAR 100,000, AN INCALCULABLE LOSS

They Were Not Simply Names on a List. They Were Us.

Numbers alone cannot possibly measure the impact of the coronavirus
on America, whether it is the number of patients treated, jobs
interrupted, or lives cut short. As the country nears a grim milestone
of 100,000 deaths attributed to the virus, The New York Times
scoured obituaries and death notices of the victims. The 1,000 people
here reflect just 1 percent of the toll. None were mere numbers.

ABOUT THIS PROJECT

The descriptions of the lives of a thousand people in the United States
who died because of the coronavirus were drawn from hundreds of
obituaries, news articles, and paid death notices that have appeared in
newspapers and digital media over the past few months. They have
been lightly edited for clarity.

They were compiled from the following publications:
Daily death data is from a New York Times database of reports from
state and local health agencies.

By Dan Barry, Larry Buchanan, Clinton Cargill, Annie Daniel, Alain Delaquérière, Lazaro Gamio, Gabriel Gianordoli, Rich Harris, Barbara Harvey, John Haskins, Jon Huang, Simone Landon, Juliette Love, Grace Maalouf, Alex Leeds Matthews, Farah Mohamed, Steven Moity, Destinée-Charisse Royal, Matt Ruby, and Eden Weingart.

Additional research by Yuriria Avila, Nicholas Bogel-Burroughs, Penn Bullock, Sophia June, Lauren Leatherby, Alex Lemonides, Denise Lu, Aimee Ortiz, Anjali Singhvi and Chi Zhang. Additional editing by Jason Bailey, Eric Morse, and Alison Peterson.

The New York Times

VOL. CLXIX ... No. 58,703   © 2020 The New York Times Company   NEW YORK, SUNDAY, MAY 24, 2020 $6.00

U.S. DEATHS NEAR 100,000, AN INCALCULABLE LOSS

They Were Not Simply Names on a List. They Were Us.

Numbers alone cannot possibly measure the impact of the coronavirus on America, whether it is the number of patients treated, jobs interrupted or lives cut short. As the country nears a grim milestone of 100,000 deaths attributed to the virus, The New York Times scoured obituaries and death notices of the victims. The 1,000 people here reflect just 1 percent of the toll. None were mere numbers.

Patricia Dowd, 57, San Jose, Calif., auditor in Silicon Valley • Marion Krueger, 65, Kirkland, Wash., great-grandmother with an easy laugh • Jermaine Ferro, 77, Lee County, Fla., wife with little time to enjoy a new marriage • Cornelius Lawyer, 84, Bellevue, Wash., sharecropper's son • Loretta Mendoza Dionisio, 68, Los Angeles, cancer survivor born in the Philippines • Patricia Frieson, 61, Chicago, former nurse • Luis Juarez, 54, Romeoville, Ill., traveled often in the United States and Mexico • Merle C. Dey, 56, Tulsa, Okla., ordained minister • Alan Lund, 81, Washington, conductor with "the most amazing ear" • Black N Mild, 44, New Orleans, bounce D.J. and radio personality • Michael Mika, 73, Chicago, Vietnam veteran • John Cofrancesco, 52, New Jersey, administrator at a nursing facility • Donald Raymond Haws, 88, Jacksonville, Fla., administered Holy Eucharist to hospital patients • Fred Walter Gray, 75, Benton County, Wash., liked his bacon and hash browns crispy • JoAnn Stokes-Smith, 87, Charleston, S.C., loved to travel and covered much of the globe • Ronald W. Lewis, 68, New Orleans, preserver of that city's performance traditions • John-Sebastian Laird-Hammond, 59, Washington, D.C., member of a Franciscan monastery • Carl Redd, 62, Chicago, squeezed in every moment he could with his only grandchild • Larry Rathgeb, 90, West Bloomfield Hills, Mich., designed the first 200-m.p.h. stock car • Alvin Elton, 56, Chicago, followed in his father's footsteps as a pipefitter • Arnold Obey, 73, San Juan, Puerto Rico, educator and marathoner • Donald J. Horsfall, 72, Rydal, Pa., co-wrote nine books about computing • Kevin Charles Patz, 54, Seattle, active in the AIDS Foundation • Mike Longo, 83, New York City, jazz pianist, composer and educator • Walter Robb, 91, New York, former General Electric Co. executive • Dave Edwards, 48, New York City, college basketball assist wizard • Dez-Ann Romain, 36, New York City, innovative high school principal • Laneska Barksdale, 47, Detroit, ballroom dancing star • Carole Brookins, 76, Palm Beach, Fla., early woman on Wall Street and a World Bank official • George Freeman Winfield, 72, Shelburne, Vt., could make anything grow • Harold L. Upjohn, 91, Burlingame, Calif., conducted clinical research at Walter Reed Army Medical Center • Terrence McNally, 81, Sarasota, Fla., Tony-winning playwright of gay life • Joseph Graham, 67, Chicago, school custodian • Theresa Elaine, 50, New Orleans, renowned for her business making detailed pins and corsages • Sterling Madden Jr., 76, Arlington, Va., developer known for his friendliness • Alan Finder, 72, Ridgewood, N.J., unflappable New York Times journalist • Floyd Cardoz, 59, Montclair, N.J., Indian chef of fine dining • Klous Kelly, 46, New York City, nurse in the Covid fight • Romi Coka, 91, New York City, saved 66 Jewish families from the Gestapo • Kenneth R. Going, 87, Grafton, Wis., Green Bay Packers season ticket holder for 50 years • Frederick Carl Harris, 70, Massachusetts, an exuberant laugh • Irvin Herman, 94, Indianapolis, Army man modest about his service in the Pacific • Ricardo Castaneda, 64, New York City, caricaturist and psychiatrist who served his patients until the end • Mark Blum, 69, New York City, Obie Award-winning stage and screen actor • Robert Earl Schaefer, 87, Seattle, radiologist, woodworker, artist and scholar • John C. West Jr., 71, Camden, S.C., avid observer and participant in South Carolina politics • Gerald Anthony Morales, 61, Louisiana, an encyclopedic knowledge of old Hollywood • Landon Spradlin, 66, Concord, N.C., preacher and blues guitarist • Maria Linda Villanueva Sun, 81, Newport News, Va., organized food programs for children in the Philippines • Susan Rokus, 73, Hamilton, Virginia, reading tutor focused on student success • Freddy Rodriguez Sr., 89, Denver, played the saxophone at Denver's oldest jazz club for 40 years • Caroline McLaurin, 86, Chicago, never at a loss for words • Peggy Rakestraw, 72, Matteson, Ill., loved reading, especially mystery novels • Wanda Bailey, 63, Crete, Ill., one of nine siblings • Rocco Patrick Ursino, 90, Bellevue, Wash., preceded in death by his wife of 65 years • Sandy Prust, 92, Bellevue, Wash., engineer forever chasing the wind • Leroy Perryman Jr., 74, Hazel Crest, Ill., ultimate entertainer • Mary Virginia McKenn, 66, Chicago, devoured art in every medium • Roger Lehne, 93, Fargo, N.D., could be a real jokester • Michael Sorkin, 71, New York City, champion of social justice through architecture • George Valentine, 66, Washington, D.C., lawyer who mentored others • James Quigley, 77, Chicago, rebel of the family • Sherman Pitman, 61, Chicago, dedicated his life to his church and his neighborhood • Susan McPherson Gottsegen, 74, Palm Beach, Fla., loyal and generous friend to many • Andreas Koutsoudakis, 59, New York City, trailblazer for TriBeCa • Bob Barnum, 64, St. Petersburg, Fla., leader in Florida Pride events • Neal Sinkiat, 64, Olney, Md., nurse planning for retirement • Thomas E. Anglin, 85, Cumming, Ga., created many wonderful memories for his family • Robert Manley Argo Jr., 75, South Bay, Calif., member of Cal Amo Flyers • Michael McKinnell, 84, Beverly, Mass., architect of Boston's monumental City Hall • Huguette Dorsey, 94, Somerville, N.J., coached several championship-winning junior high girls basketball teams • Lynne Sierra, 68, Roselle, Ill., grandmother who was always full of ideas • Louvenia Henderson, 44, Tonawanda, N.Y., proud single mother of three • Carol Sue Rubin, 69, West Bloomfield, Mich., loved travel, mahjong and crossword puzzles • Marion Lucille Kujda, 92, Royal Oak, Mich., would use chalk and oil paints to capture family portraits • Alice Chawdarian, 92, Michigan, loving, generous and adventurous spirit • Bassey Offiong, 25, Michigan, saw friends at their worst but brought out their best • Bobby Joseph Hebert, 81, Cut Off, La., a 33-year career with the Louisiana Department of Transportation • Minette Goff Cooper, 70, Louisiana, loved big and told people she loved them all the time • Jéssica Beatriz Cortez, 32, Los Angeles, immigrated to the United States three years ago • Marie Caronia, 84, Inwood, N.Y., iconic figure in the Inwood community • April Dunn, 33, Baton Rouge, La., advocate for disability rights • Cedric Dixon, 48, New York City, police detective in Harlem with a gift for interrogation • William Helmreich, 74, Great Neck, N.Y., sociologist who walked New York City • Harvy Bayard, 68, New York, grew up directly across the street from the old Yankee Stadium • Maxwell M. Mozell, 90, Syracuse, N.Y., founded the Association for Chemoreception Sciences • Timothy J. Liszewski, 60, Columbia, S.C., active member of the South Carolina Progressive Network • Eastern Stewart Jr., 71, Annapolis, Md., veteran with a gift for peacemaking • Freda Ocran, 51, New York City, nurse with a zest for travel and knowledge • Douglas Hickok, 57, Pennsylvania, military's first virus casualty • Luiza Ogorodnik, 84, Skokie, Ill., emigrated from Ukraine • Thomas A. Real, 81, Newtown, Pa., was at peace on his Harley • Julian Anguiano-Maya, 51, Chicago, life of the party • Sandra Piotrowski, 77, Tinley Park, Ill., worked as a meat-cutter for Jewel supermarkets • Robert Stan, 68, Greensburg, Ind., competitive athlete, up until his last years • Melvin Pumphrey, 80, Chicago Heights, Ill., relished his role as a mentor • Angel Escamilla, 67, Naperville, Ill., assistant pastor • Marguerite M. Horgus, 85, Sweetgrass, Mont., her hospitality was known throughout Toole County and beyond • Joseph Micajah Thomas II, 88, New York City, represented theatrical, TV and movie personalities • Beryl Bornay, 94, New York City, actress and children's TV host • John Joseph Reed Jr., 74, Edmonds, Wash., passionate about retaining his town's small-town atmosphere • Sidney Siegel, 92, Woodbury, N.Y., pioneer in the promotional products industry • Robert M. Weintraub, 96, New York, a long career in the import-export business • Joe Diffie, 61, Nashville, Grammy-winning country music star • Herman Boelan, 86, Florida, retired architect always eager to travel • Horace Saunders, 96, Mount Airy, Md., tailor • Gary Holmberg, 77, Mount Airy, Md., retired firefighter • Chad Capule, 49, Fond du Lac, Wis., I.T. project manager remembered for his love of trivia • Robert Garff, 77, Utah, former speaker of the Utah House, auto executive and philanthropist • Phillip Thomas, 48, Chicago, his Walmart co-workers were like family • Alan Merrill, 69, New York City, songwriter of "I Love Rock 'n' Roll" • Peter Sakas, 67, Northbrook, Ill., ran an animal hospital • Joseph Yaggi, 66, Indiana, mentor and friend to many • Mary Roman, 84, Norwalk, Conn., shot-put champion and fixture in local politics • Lorena Borjas, 59, New York City, transgender immigrant activist • James I. Goodrich, 73, New York City, surgeon who separated conjoined twins • Janice Preschel, 60, Teaneck, N.J., founded a food pantry • Jean-Claude Henrion, 72, Atlantis, Fla., always rode Harley-Davidsons • Joseph J. Deren Jr., 75, Turners Falls, Mass., retired meter-reader • Gerald Cassidy, 66, Peachtree Corners, Ga., owner of Shamrock Salvage & Appraisal Inc. • David Reissig, 82, Vermont, retired from the U.S. Customs Agency after 28 years • Angelo Piro, 87, New York City, known for serenading friends with Tony Bennett songs • Sandra Lee deBlecourt, 61, Maryland, loved taking care of people • Jose Vazquez, 51, Chicago, husband and father • Alberto Castro, 85, Melrose Park, Ill., made time to create and listen to music • Jerry Manley, 58, Prince Frederick, Md., retired police sergeant • Wallace Roney, 59, Paterson, N.J., jazz trumpet virtuoso • Cristina, 64, New York City, downtown New York singer with a cult following • Robert H. Westphal, 75, Fond du Lac, Wis., statesman in the construction industry • Clair Dunlap, 89, Washington, pilot still teaching people to fly at 88 • Marylou Armer, 43, Sonoma Valley, Calif., veteran police detective • Regina D. Cullen, 81, Shrewsbury, Mass., small in stature but strong in spirit • Sanden Santos-Vizcaino, 54, New York City, beloved public school teacher • Frank Gabrio, 60, New York City, emergency room doctor who died in husband's arms • Sterling E. Matthews, 60, Midlothian, Va., cancer survivor who served as a deacon • Alby Kass, 89, California, lead singer of a Yiddish folk group • Roger Eckart, 78, Indiana, retired firefighter and old-school barber • Martin Douglas, 71, New York City, maestro of a steel-pan band • Daniel Spector, 68, Memphis, mentor to other Memphis artists • Mary Minervini, 91, Oak Lawn, Ill., sign-language interpreter • Salomon S. Podgursky, 84, Morristown, N.J., loved to figure out how things worked • Dale E. Thurman, 66, Lexington, Ky., tailor known for his exacting work and strong opinions • Ellis Marsalis, 85, New Orleans, jazz pianist and patriarch of a family of musicians • Richard Passman, 94, Silver Spring, Md., rocket engineer in the early days of supersonic flight • David Driskell, 88, Hyattsville, Md., champion of African-American art • Bucky Pizzarelli, 94, Saddle River, N.J., master of jazz guitar • Tarlach MacNiallais, 57, New York City, Belfast-born fighter for L.B.G.T. and disability rights • Antonio Checo, 67, New York City, social worker • Albert Petrocelli, 73, New York City, fire chief who answered the call on 9/11 • Adam Schlesinger, 52, Poughkeepsie, N.Y., songwriter for rock, film and the stage • Frederick Brown Starr, 87, Greensboro, N.C., liked the mental challenges of business • Douglas Alan Roberts, 69, Vancouver, Wash., authority on aviation • Muriel M. Going, 92, Cedarburg, Wis., taught her girls sheepshead and canasta • Beverly Collins, 83, Portland, Maine, longtime registered nurse and hospital volunteer • Scott Melter, 60, Wyoming, Minn., worked as an engineer with Comcast • Florencio Almazo Morán, 65, New York City, one-man army • Jennifer Robin Arnold, 67, New York City, Broadway costume dresser • John Nakawatase, 82, Lincolnwood, Ill., coach and Scout leader • Jesus Roman Melendez, 49, New York, famous in family circles for his birria beef stew • Ralph Plaisance, 87, Massapequa, N.Y., "we called him the Grand Poobah" • Audrey Malone, 68, Chicago, sang gospel music as a member of the Malone Sisters • Terrence George Driscoll, 87, Plymouth, Mich., father figure • Luchs Hall, 97, Chicago, dubbed the "pistol-packing preacher" • Ronnie Estes, 73, Stevensville, Md., always wanted to be near the ocean • Anita Fial, 87, New York City, marketing expert who brought exotic foods to green grocers • Patricia Bosworth, 86, New York City, actress who wrote biographies of famous friends • Azade Kilic, 69, New York, two-time cancer survivor • Marco DiFranco, 50, Chicago, police officer who was never at a loss for words • John E. Broadly, 84, Scituate, Mass., honored to march with the American Legion in many parades • Julia Maye Alexander, 81, Upland, Calif., taught math, English and history for over 30 years • Bruce W. Sowalski, 68, Sand Lake, N.Y., found his special place at Big Bowman Pond • Samuel Kramer, 91, Potomac, Md., congregation's founding member • Sean Boynes, 44, Annapolis, Md., pharmacy manager with young daughters • Norma Hoza, 101, Wilmette, Ill., mom to six sons • Nancy Ferguson, 77, Chicago, true community activist • Harry J. Hayes, 96, Fort Wright, Ky., original member of the Navy's elite Underwater Demolition Team • Glenn Daniel Bellitto, 62, New York, town councilman • Robert Lee Amos, 66, Columbus, Ind., expert marksman and firearms instructor • Luis Fitzpatrick, 85, Bolton, Ill., part of a tightknit family • Judith Plotkin-Goldberg, 88, Massachusetts, noted voiceover artist for radio and TV • Coby Adolph, 44, Chicago, entrepreneur and adventurer • Steven J. Huber, 64, Jefferson City, Mo., loved creating perfect smiles • Charles Miles, 72, Chatham, Ill., retired therapist and mentor • Don Whan, 67, Indiana, sports fan who loved Purdue University • Albert K. Webster, 82, New York City, executive behind New York Philharmonic's economic growth • Kevin Masterson, 74, New York City, joined Goldman Sachs in 1976 • Randy G. Addison, 64, Carrollton, Ga., survived being shot in the line of duty in 1984 • Ronald Willenkamp, 75, Wisconsin, proud to have logged over five million miles behind the wheel • Lloyd Paul Leftwich, 91, Louisiana, inveterate harmonica player • Helen Molina, 85, Washington, all-around supporter of the Washington Huskies • Ronald Burdette Culp, 84, Redding, Calif., helped countless people by providing housing and support • Norman Walker, 80, China Township, Mich., shared his produce with food pantries and his neighbors • Peter Bainum, 82, Bethesda, Md., former aerospace engineering professor at Howard University • Ann Kolb, 78, New York, leader in integrating schools • Helen Kafkis, 91, Chicago, known for her Greek chicken and stuffed peppers • John A. [continued], New York City, veterinarian who served Harlem • Lila A. Fenwick, 87, New York City, first black woman to graduate from Harvard Law School • Vincent Lionti, 60, New York City, Met Opera violist and youth orchestra conductor • Ann Youngerman Smoler, 87, New York City, had a passion for social justice • Thomas Waters, 56, New York City, armed the affordable housing movement with data and analysis • Luke Workoff, 33, Huntington, N.Y., his relentless passion was for his family and friends • José Díaz-Ayala, 38, Palm Beach, Fla., served with the Palm Beach County Sheriff's Office for 14 years • Antonio Nieves, 73, Chicago, always seemed to be busy with some home project • Jeanne Hammond Byrnes, 97, Danbury, Conn., received numerous awards for her accounting skills • Alice Coopersmith Furst, 87, Kentfield, Calif., in the first class of girls admitted to the Bronx High School of Science • Bobby Lee Barber, 84, Buckley, Wash., Seahawks season-ticket holder • Thomas A. Adamavich, 78, Sheboygan, Wis., especially proud of his Lithuanian heritage • Kyra Swartz, 33, New York, volunteered for pet rescue organizations • Rhoda Hatch, 73, Chicago, first in her family to graduate college • Regina Dix-Parsons, 75, Schenectady, N.Y., stalwart church gospel singer • Lakisha Willis White, 45, Orlando, Fla., was helping to raise some of her dozen grandchildren • Barbara Yazbeck Vethacke, 74, St. Clair Shores, Mich., she was known to many as Babs • June Beverly Hill, 85, Sacramento, no one made creamed potatoes or fried sweet corn the way she did • Kimarlee Nguyen, 33, Everett, Mass., writer who inspired her Brooklyn high school students • Kamal Ahmed, 69, New York City, hotel banquet worker and Bangladeshi leader • Raymond Copeland, 46, New York City, sanitation worker living his fullest days • Israel Sauz, 22, Broken Arrow, Okla., new father • Lester Eber, 82, New York, worked for over six decades in the wine and liquor industry • Harry P. Misthos, 87, San Francisco Bay Area, Calif., loved the ocean and enjoyed swimming and boating • Leo Sreebny, 98, Seattle, preferred bolo ties to neckties, suspenders to belts • Robert Barghaan, 88, New York City, could fix almost anything • Patricia H. Thatcher, 79, Clifton Park, N.Y., sang in her church choir for 42 years • Howard Alexander Nelson Jr., 84, New Orleans, strong advocate for health care policy • Allan Joseph Dickson Jr., 67, New Jersey, loved the Jersey Shore music scene • John Cassano, 70, Palos Park, Ill., family jokester • Eugene Lamar Limbrick, 41, Colorado Springs, loved automobiles, especially trucks • Jim J. Wolf Sr., 72, South Holland, Ill., known as "Big Wolf" to the basketball players he coached • Robert LeBlanc, 87, Cambridge, Mass., worked in construction and served in the Army • Antoinette Marie Lutz, 91, Chester, Conn., candy striper at St. Raphael's Hospital • Vincent G. Frainee, 68, Redlands, Calif., owned Frainee Water Trucks for 44 years • Andrew Kowalczyk, 63, Coral Gables, Fla., a heart of service • Jana Prince, 43, Gretna, La., social worker who dedicated her life to others • Joseph Migliucci, 81, White Plains, N.Y., fourth-generation owner of Mario's restaurant, a Bronx institution • Reuben Gutoff, 92, New York City, founded Strategy Associates • Gerard Rosenberg, 85, New York City, retired New York Supreme Court justice • Marty Derer, 56, New Jersey, loved to referee basketball games • Harold Reisner, 78, Pittsburgh, took furniture repair to the level of an art form • Clark Osojnicki, 56, Stillwater, Minn., well known in the world of agility dog training • Kevin John Cahill, 83, New York City, directed Alba House Cornerstone Bookstore in lower Manhattan • Janissa Delacruz, 31, Haverstraw, N.Y., known for having a smile on her face • Clifford J. Williams, 81, Schaghticoke, N.Y., member for over 46 years of the Operating Engineers Union, Local No. 106 • Robert L. Crahen, 87, Waunakee, Wis., nicknamed "Boxcar Bob" for his luck in shaking dice • Elizabeth Batista, 57, Waterbury, Conn., unwavering faith and dedication to the Catholic Church • Timothy Brunscomb, 32, Chicago, always busy looking out for others • Paul Warech, 86, Vineland, N.J., widely surmised he could have played Major League Baseball • Marlon Alston, 46, Chicago, bus driver and school security guard • Hailey Herrera, 25, New York City, budding therapist with a gift for empathy • James V. Walsh, 76, New Jersey, volunteered his time to church car raffles, fund-raisers and picnics • Lindas Karolis Mikalonis, 86, Berkley, Mich., immigrated to New York from a German refugee camp after World War II • Gene Zahas, 78, Oakland, Calif., fierce advocate for educational opportunity • Mario Araujo, 49, Chicago, Chicago firefighter • William D. Greeke, 55, Massachusetts, thought it was important to know a person's life story • Beatrice Rubin, 96, New Jersey, her size belied her strength and spirit • Jack Butler, 78, Indiana, lived in the house he grew up in • Susan Grey Hopp Crofoot, 97, Westwood, N.J., took great joy in writing little ditties under her pen name, Penelope Penwiper • James David Gewirtzman, 72, New City, N.Y., spent some of his happiest hours hiking in the Adirondacks • Henry E. Graff, 98, Greenwich, Conn., Columbia University historian of U.S. presidents • Marj Jo Davitto, 82, Thornton, Ill., people were her hobby • Yaakov Perlow, 89, New York City, leader of the Novominsker Hasidic dynasty • Joseph F. Kelly, 81, New York City, did two tours through the Panama Canal to Antarctica • John Prine, 73, Nashville, country-folk singer who was a favorite of Bob Dylan • Perry Buchalter, 63, Florida, quiet hero • Monica Maley, 74, Rehoboth Beach, Del., loved animals, had dogs and cats, and rode horses • Thomas Tarbell Russell, 83, Longmeadow, Mass., mentored by the computer science pioneer Grace Hopper • Ruth Skapinok, 85, Roseville, Calif., backyard birds were known to eat from her hand • Faralyn Havir, 92, Minnesota, her favorite thing was meeting new people • Torrin Jamal Howard, 26, Waterbury, Conn., gentle giant, athlete and musician • James O'Brien Johnson, 74, Joplin, Mo., pastor of Mt. Sinai Church of God in Christ • Joseph W. Hammond, 64, Chicago, stopped working to look after his aging parents • Morris Loeb, 90, Northbrook, Ill., endlessly curious, never really finished • Dante Dennis Flagello, 62, Rome, Ga., his greatest accomplishment was his relationship with his wife • Tommie Adams, 71, Chicago, moved antiques for more than 25 years • Myra Helen Robinson, 57, Detroit, more adept than many knew • Roger Mckinney-Wagner, 73, Lowell, Mass., professor at the Salter School • Sean Christian Keville, 47, New Providence, N.J., enjoyed talking sports with family • John Herman Ciomax, Jr., 62, Newark, one of the few African-American corporate bond traders on Wall Street • José Torres, 73, New York City, restaurateur favored by salsa music's stars • Stuart Cohen, 73, New York City, Brooklyn cabbie who found a home in Buddhism • Johnnie D. Veasley, 76, Country Club Hills, Ill., teacher's aide • Mary M. Desole, 93, Poughkeepsie, N.Y., member of the Literacy Volunteers of America • Vera Flint, 97, Beverly, Mass., face behind the counter at a family-owned grocery store • Mike Field, 59, Valley Stream, N.Y., first responder during the 9/11 attacks • Chianti Jackson Harpool, 51, Baltimore, social worker and then a political fundraiser • Conrad Duncker, 99, Chicago, longtime dentist • Peter Kafkis, 91, Chicago, worked mostly factory jobs to support his family • Clara Louise Bennett, 91, Albany, Ga., sang her grandchildren a song on the first day of school each year • Ilona Murai Kerman, 96, New York, featured in multiple Broadway productions • Mauricio Valdivia, 52, Chicago, wanted everyone to feel welcome • Robert Dugal, 58, Oak Park, Ill., advocate for others with disabilities • Sharyn Lynn Vogel, 74, Aurora, Colo., photographer, gourmet cook, sparkling hostess and traveler • Robert Charles Bazzell, 88, Novi, Mich., helped drive the family car along Route 66 • Claudia Obermiller, 73, Nebraska, deep-hearted country girl • Reggie Bagala, 54, Lockport, La., Republican freshman in the state Legislature • Richard Joseph Lenihan Jr., 55, Pearl River, N.Y., man of faith and a proud Irish-American • Deyroll Arteaga, 66, Central Valley, N.Y., made friends everywhere he went • Estelle Kestenbaum, 91, Leonia, N.J., secretary to a New Jersey judge • Artemis Nazarian, 88, Englewood Cliffs, N.J., opened a Los Angeles preschool • Myles Coker, 69, New York City, freed from life in prison • Richard Alexander Ross Jr., 66, Boynton Beach, Fla., lifelong karate instructor • Helen Boles Days, 96, Wynnewood, Pa., made what she had work for her • Marcus Edward Cooper Jr., 83, Louisiana, he loved his wife and said, "Yes, dear" a lot • Nelson Perdomo, 44, Middlesex County, N.J., veteran corrections officer and father of three • Rosemarie Amerosi, 87, New York City, retired bank teller • Timothy H. Gray, 66, Orleans, Ind., worked for the Orange County Highway Department • Tommie Brown, 79, Gary, Ind., security worker who died the same day as his wife • Doris Brown, 79, Gary, Ind., wife who died on the same day as her husband • Marie Scanlan Walker, 99, Louisiana, never drew attention to herself • Frances M. Pilot, 81, Wall, N.J., known as Big Momma to all who loved her • George J. Foerst Jr., 99, New Jersey, called "The Captain" by friends and family • John B. Ahrens, 96, Newton, Mass., lifelong pacifist • Parker Knoll, 68, Indiana, a decades-long career in ministry • Kerri Ann Kennedy-Tompkins, 48, Garrison, N.Y., worked as a special education teacher for many years • Rosemarie Franzese, 70, Nevada, former hairstylist and avid New York Yankees fan • Bernard David Seckler, 95, Newton, Mass., math reader for Recordings for the Blind • Samuel Hargress Jr., 84, New York City, owner of Paris Blues, a beloved Harlem jazz joint • Michael Lee Jordan, 69, McLeansville, N.C., retired from Sears Outlet Stores as an assistant manager • Merrick Dowson, 67, San Francisco Bay Area, Calif., nothing delighted him more than picking up the bill • Wesley Richard Fahrbach II, 69, Fremont, Ohio, known throughout Ohio for his knowledge of local history • Harley E. Acker, 79, Troupsburg, N.Y., discovered his true calling when he started driving a school bus • Ariola Rawis, 81, Chicago, caretaker of her neighborhood • Roger Liddell, 65, Flint, Mich., brought smiles to everyone he interacted with • Luther Coleman, 108, Evergreen Park, Ill., man who seemed to know everything • Denise Camille Buczek, 72, Bristol, Conn., loved writing birthday and holiday cards, poems and lists • Charles Constantino, 86, Menlo Park, N.J., worked 40 years for The New York Times • Ben Doherty, 83, Boston, stockbroker who founded Doherty Financial Services • John Horton Conway, 82, New Brunswick, N.J., mathematician known as the "magical genius" • Stanley Chera, 77, New York City, developer and friend of the president • Robby Browne, 72, New York City, Realtor and philanthropist who socialized with celebrities • Wynn Handman, 97, New York City, acting teacher and a founder of the American Place Theater • Adam Kovacs, 72, New York City, cartoonist and an expert on musicals • Peter Brown, 53, New Jersey, manager of the S.W. Brown & Son Funeral Home • Irene Gasior, 94, Pennsylvania, great-grandmother with a flair for pizzelles • Stanley L. Morse, 88, Stark County, Ohio, trombonist who once turned down an offer to join Duke Ellington's orchestra • Margaret Laughlin, 91, Massachusetts, had a mystic's direct sense of wonder and oneness • Cynthia Whiting, 66, La Plata, Md., retiree determined to spoil her granddaughter • Steve Joltin, 75, Rockville, Md., I.T. manager with "an eye for beautiful and unusual things" • Gerald Glenn, 66, Richmond, Va., police officer turned pastor • Maclear Jacoby Jr., 93, Washington, D.C., inspiring math teacher • Doris Mae Burkhart Kale, 98, Pennsylvania, excelled in the kitchen • Josephine Posnanski, 98, New Jersey, loved to dance • Phil Langley, 83, Frankfort, Ill., member of Harness Racing Hall of Fame • Vinton Timely Mason, 86, Beaumont, Mich., co-owned the Bark-and-All logging company • Maria Garcia-Rodelo, 52, Nevada, would walk her children to school every morning • Fernando Mitoff, 60, New York City, graffiti artist with a generous spirit • John Watson, 73, Philadelphia, anywhere he went, he took pictures • Joyce Posson Winston, 93, North Bergen, N.J., editor at the Ladies' Home Journal • John B. Lynch, 76, Wilmington, Mass., lifelong educator • Orlando Moncada, 56, Bronxville, N.Y., left Peru and grabbed hold of the American dream • John Schoffstall, 41, Terre Haute, Ind., volunteer youth football coach • Theodore Gaffney, 92, Washington, D.C., photographer of the Freedom Riders • Alan A. Potanka, 68, Berlin, Conn., collector of stamps and coins • Harold Davis Jr., 63, Chicago, radio host and youth advocate • Michael Giangrande Sr., 78, Bellmore, N.Y., "Mayor of Martin Avenue" • Timothy Ross, 68, Michigan, worked more than 30 years for General Motors • Sherroll Stokes, 54, Chicago, active in her church • Larry Jones, 61, Chicago, longtime high school referee • Shirley S. D'Stefan, 90, Florham Park, N.J., reader of books on birds and other wildlife • Billy Ross, 53, Milwaukee, staff member and mentor at the Milwaukee Rescue Mission • Helen Silvia, 96, Brockton, Mass., known as the "fashionista" in her nursing home • Davis Begays, 48, Cudei, N.M., worked at the Home Depot • Rose Mary Infantino, 88, Rye Brook, N.Y., daughter of Italian immigrants • Ann Sullivan, 91, Woodland Hills, Calif., animator for Disney films, including "The Little Mermaid" • Norman Gulamerian, 92, New Providence, N.J., art supply businessman with a romantic streak • Kenneth L. Jewel, 78, Mountain Lakes, N.J., exceptional radiologist • Jerzy Glowczewski, 97, New York City, last of the WWII Polish fighter pilots • Joan M. Heaney, 77, Upper Brookville, N.Y., built the family heating-oil business into a successful company • Delia Regina DiTullio, 91, Jamaica Plain, Mass., always put her children first • Joanne Stone Rusnak, 84, Endicott, N.Y., classy lady with style and elegance • Anita Robinson, 94, Minnesota, shared her knowledge and love of reading • William U. Roulette III, 93, Stroudsburg, Pa., enjoyed being a waterman on his work boat on Chesapeake Bay • Antoinette Meyer, 95, Crownsville, Md., trailblazing deputy sheriff • Michael Wrotalak Jr., 92, Glen Cove, N.Y., brought the family to church every week • Marvin L. Thomas, 81, Sun Lakes, Ariz., a million-dollar smile • Edmon C. Carmichael, 79, Detroit, pillar in the Detroit community • Linda Nute, 61, Hazel Crest, Ill., home helper for many years • Lela Reed, 95, Country Club Hills, Ill., babysitter for the local church • Joan Cecile Berngen, 69, Burbank, Ill., known for her amazing sense of humor • Gwendolyn A. Carmichael, 72, Detroit, definition of love, loyalty, and the ability to serve others • James Lowell Miller Jr., 64, Cedar Rapids, Iowa, known as the bonfire builder • Dolores A. Vail, 89, Torrington, Conn., her hobbies included reading, especially

Continued on Page 12

1 Auditor in Silicon Valley. *Patricia Dowd, 57, San Jose, Calif.*

2 Great-grandmother with an easy laugh. *Marion Krueger, 85, Kirkland, Wash.*

3 Wife with little time to enjoy a new marriage. *Jermaine Ferro, 77, Lee County, Fla.*

4 Sharecropper's son. *Cornelius Lawyer, 84, Bellevue, Wash.*

5 Cancer survivor born in the Philippines. *Loretta Mendoza Dionisio, 68, Los Angeles*

6 Former nurse. *Patricia Frieson, 61, Chicago*

7 Ordained minister. *Merle C. Dry, 55, Tulsa, Okla.*

8 Traveled often in the United States and Mexico. *Luis Juarez, 54, Romeoville, Ill.*

9 Vietnam veteran. *Michael Mika, 73, Chicago*

10 Bounce D.J. and radio personality. *Black N Mild, 44, New Orleans*

11 Administered Holy Eucharist to hospital patients. *Donald Raymond Haws, 88, Jacksonville, Fla.*

12 Conductor with "the most amazing ear." *Alan Lund, 81, Washington*

13 Administrator at a nursing facility. *John Cofrancesco, 52, New Jersey*

14 Liked his bacon and hash browns crispy. *Fred Walter Gray, 75, Benton County, Wash.*

15 Loved to travel and covered much of the globe. *JoAnn Stokes-Smith, 87, Charleston, S.C.*

16 Preserver of the city's performance traditions. *Ronald W. Lewis, 68, New Orleans*

17 Member of a Franciscan monastery. *John-Sebastian Laird-Hammond, 59, Washington, D.C.*

18 Squeezed in every moment he could with his only grandchild. *Carl Redd, 62, Chicago*

19 Jazz pianist, composer and educator. *Mike Longo, 83, New York City*

20 Engineer behind the first 200-m.p.h. stock car. *Larry Rathgeb, 90, West Bloomfield Hills, Mich.*

21 Followed in his father's footsteps as a pipefitter. *Alvin Elton, 56, Chicago*

22 Co-wrote nine books about computing. *Donald J. Horsfall, 72, Rydal, Pa.*

23 Educator and marathoner. *Arnold Obey, 73, San Juan, P.R.*

24 Active in the AIDS Foundation. *Kevin Charles Patz, 64, Seattle*

25 Former General Electric Co. executive. *Walter Robb, 91, New York*

26 Early woman on Wall Street and a World Bank official. *Carole Brookins, 76, Palm Beach, Fla.*

27 College basketball assist wizard. *Dave Edwards, 48, New York City*

28 Could make anything grow. *George Freeman Winfield, 72, Shelburne, Vt.*

29 Innovative high school principal. *Dez-Ann Romain, 36, New York City*

30 Ballroom dancing star. *Laneeka Barksdale, 47, Detroit*

31 Conducted clinical research at Walter Reed Army Medical Center. *Harold L. Upjohn, 91, Burlingame, Calif.*

32 Green Bay Packers season ticket holder for fifty years. *Kenneth R. Going, 87, Grafton, Wis.*

33 Renowned for her business making detailed pins and corsages. *Theresa Elloie, 63, New Orleans*

34 Developer known for his friendliness. *Sterling Maddox Jr., 78, Arlington, Va.*

35 School custodian and steppin' aficionado. *Joseph Graham, 67, Chicago*

36 Tony-winning playwright of gay life. *Terrence McNally, 81, Sarasota, Fla.*

37 Unflappable New York Times journalist. *Alan Finder, 72, Ridgewood, N.J.*

38 Indian chef of fine dining. *Floyd Cardoz, 59, Montclair, N.J.*

39 Nurse in the Covid fight. *Kious Kelly, 48, New York City*

40 Saved 56 Jewish families from the Gestapo. *Romi Cohn, 91, New York City*

41 Organized food programs for children in the Philippines. *Maria Linda Villanueva Sun, 61, Newport News, Va.*

42 Army man modest about his service in the Pacific. *Irvin Hernan, 94, Indianapolis*

43 Obie Award-winning stage and screen actor. *Mark Blum, 69, New York City*

44 Radiologist, woodworker, artist and scholar. *Robert Earl Schaefer, 87, Seattle*

45 Avid observer and participant in South Carolina politics. *John C. West Jr., 71, Camden, S.C.*

46 An encyclopedic knowledge of old Hollywood. *Gerald Anthony Morales, 91, Louisiana*

47 Preacher and blues guitarist. *Landon Spradlin, 66, Concord, N.C.*

48 Caricaturist and psychiatrist who served his patients until the end. *Ricardo Castaneda, 64, New York City*

49 Reading tutor focused on student success. *Susan Rokus, 73, Hamilton, Va.*

50 An exuberant laugh. *Frederick Carl Harris, 70, Massachusetts*

51 One of nine siblings. *Wanda Bailey, 63, Crete, Ill.*

52 Loved reading, especially mystery novels. *Peggy Rakestraw, 72, Matteson, Ill.*

53 Played the saxophone at Denver's oldest jazz club for forty years. *Freddy Rodriguez Sr., 89, Denver*

54 Never at a loss for words. *Christine McLaurin, 86, Chicago*

55 Ultimate entertainer. *Leroy Perryman Jr., 74, Hazel Crest, Ill.*

56 Champion of social justice through architecture. *Michael Sorkin, 71, New York City*

57 Devoured art in every medium. *Mary Virginia McKeon, 65, Chicago*

58 Could be a real jokester. *Roger Lehne, 93, Fargo, N.D.*

59 Engineer forever chasing the wind. *Sandy Pratt, 92, Bellevue, Wash.*

60 Preceded in death by his wife of 65 years. *Rocco Patrick Ursino, 90, Bellevue, Wash.*

61 Member of Del Amo Flyers. *Robert Manley Argo Jr., 75, South Bay, Calif.*

62 Architect of Boston's monumental City Hall. *Michael McKinnell, 84, Beverly, Mass.*

63 Created many wonderful memories for his family. *Thomas E. Anglin, 85, Cumming, Ga.*

64 Trailblazer for TriBeCa. *Andreas Koutsoudakis, 59, New York City*

65 Leader in Florida Pride events. *Bob Barnum, 64, St. Petersburg, Fla.*

66 Nurse planning for retirement. *Noel Sinkiat, 64, Olney, Md.*

67 Lawyer who mentored others. *George Valentine, 66, Washington, D.C.*

68 Rebel of the family. *James Quigley, 77, Chicago*

69 Dedicated his life to his church and his neighborhood. *Sherman Pittman, 61, Chicago*

70 Proud single mother of three. *Louvenia Henderson, 44, Tonawanda, N.Y.*

71 Grandmother who was always full of ideas. *Lynne Sierra, 68, Roselle, Ill.*

72 Coached several championship-winning junior high girls basketball teams. *Huguette Dorsey, 94, Somerville, N.J.*

73 Loyal and generous friend to many. *Susan McPherson Gottsegen, 74, Palm Beach, Fla.*

74 Grew up directly across the street from the old Yankee Stadium. *Harvey Bayard, 88, New York*

75 Loved travel, mahjong and crossword puzzles. *Carol Sue Rubin, 69, West Bloomfield, Mich.*

76 Loving, generous, and adventurous spirit. *Alice Chavdarian, 92, Michigan*

77 Saw friends at their worst but brought out their best. *Bassey Offiong, 25, Michigan*

78 Worked as a meat-cutter for Jewel supermarkets. *Sandra Piotrowski, 77, Tinley Park, Ill.*

79 Competitive athlete, up until his last years. *Robert Rust, 88, Greensburg, Ind.*

80 Immigrated to the United States three years ago. *Jéssica Beatriz Cortez, 32, Los Angeles*

81 Iconic figure in the Inwood community. *Marie Caronia, 84, Inwood, N.Y.*

82 Advocate for disability rights. *April Dunn, 33, Baton Rouge, La.*

83 Police detective in Harlem with a gift for interrogation. *Cedric Dixon, 48, New York City*

84 Sociologist who walked New York City. *William Helmreich, 74, Great Neck, N.Y.*

85 Would use chalk and oil paints to capture family portraits. *Marion Lucille Kujda, 92, Royal Oak, Mich.*

86 Founded the Association for Chemoreception Sciences. *Maxwell M. Mozell, 90, Syracuse, N.Y.*

87 Active member of the South Carolina Progressive Network. *Timothy J. Liszewski, 60, Columbia, S.C.*

88 Veteran with a gift for peacemaking. *Eastern Stewart Jr., 71, Annapolis, Md.*

89 Nurse with a zest for travel and knowledge. *Freda Ocran, 51, New York City*

90 Military's first virus casualty. *Douglas Hickok, 57, Pennsylvania*

91 Emigrated from Ukraine. *Luiza Ogorodnik, 84, Skokie, Ill.*

92 Life of the party. *Julian Anguiano-Maya, 51, Chicago*

93 Was at peace on his Harley. *Thomas A. Real, 61, Newtown, Pa.*

94 Loved big and told people she loved them all the time. *Minette Goff Cooper, 79, Louisiana*

95 A thirty-three-year career with the Louisiana Department of Transportation. *Bobby Joseph Hebert, 81, Cut Off, La.*

96 Relished his role as a mentor. *Melvin Pumphrey, 80, Chicago Heights, Ill.*

97 Assistant pastor. *Angel Escamilla, 67, Naperville, Ill.*

98 Her hospitality was known throughout Toole County and beyond. *Marguerite M. Horgus, 86, Sweetgrass, Mont.*

99 Represented theatrical, TV and movie personalities. *Joseph Micajah Thomas II, 88, New York City*

100 Actress and children's TV host. *Beryl Bernay, 94, New York City*

101 Songwriter of "I Love Rock 'n' Roll."n*Alan Merrill, 69, New York City*

102 **Pioneer in the promotional products industry.** *Sidney Siegel, 92, Woodbury, N.Y.*

103 **Passionate about retaining his town's small-town atmosphere.** *John Joseph Reed Jr., 74, Edmonds, Wash.*

104 **Grammy-winning country music star.** *Joe Diffie, 61, Nashville*

105 **Retired architect always eager to travel.** *Herman Boehm, 86, Florida*

106 **Tailor.** *Horace Saunders, 96, Mount Airy, Md.*

107 **Retired firefighter.** *Gary Holmberg, 77, Mount Airy, Md.*

108 **I.T. project manager remembered for his love of trivia.** *Chad Capule, 49, Fond du Lac, Wis.*

109 **Former speaker of the Utah House, auto executive and philanthropist.** *Robert Garff, 77, Utah*

110 **His Walmart co-workers were like family.** *Phillip Thomas, 48, Chicago*

111 **A long career in the import-export business.** *Robert M. Weintraub, 96, New York*

112 **Ran an animal hospital.** *Peter Sakas, 67, Northbrook, Ill.*

113 **Mentor and friend to many.** *Joseph Yaggi, 65, Indiana*

114 **Shot-put champion and fixture in local politics.** *Mary Roman, 84, Norwalk, Conn.*

115 **Transgender immigrant activist.** *Lorena Borjas, 59, New York City*

116 **Surgeon who separated conjoined twins.** *James T. Goodrich, 73, New York City*

117 **Founded a food pantry.** *Janice Preschel, 60, Teaneck, N.J.*

118 **Always rode Harley-Davidsons.** *Jean-Claude Henrion, 72, Atlantis, Fla.*

119 **Retired meter-reader.** *Joseph J. Deren Jr., 75, Turners Falls, Mass.*

120 **Owner of Shamrock Salvage & Appraisal Inc.** *Gerald Cassidy, 66, Peachtree Corners, Ga.*

121 **Retired from the U.S. Customs Agency after 28 years.** *David Reissig, 82, Vermont*

122 **Known for serenading friends with Tony Bennett songs.** *Angelo Piro, 87, New York City*

123 **Loved taking care of people.** *Sandra Lee deBlecourt, 61, Maryland*

124 **Husband and father.** *Jose Vazquez, 51, Chicago*

125 **Made time to create and listen to music.** *Alberto Castro, 86, Melrose Park, Ill.*

126 **Retired police sergeant.** *Jerry Manley, 58, Prince Frederick, Md.*

127 **Jazz trumpet virtuoso.** *Wallace Roney, 59, Paterson, N.J.*

128 **Downtown New York singer with a cult following.** *Cristina, 64, New York City*

129 **Statesman in the construction industry.** *Robert H. Westphal, 75, Fond du Lac, Wis.*

130 **Pilot still teaching people to fly at eighty-eight.** *Clair Dunlap, 89, Washington*

131 **Veteran police detective.** *Marylou Arner, 43, Sonoma Valley, Calif.*

132 **Small in stature but strong in spirit.** *Regina D. Cullen, 81, Shrewsbury, Mass.*

133 **Beloved public-school teacher.** *Sandra Santos-Vizcaino, 54, New York City*

134 **Emergency room doctor who died in husband's arms.** *Frank Gabrin, 60, New York City*

135 **Cancer survivor who served as a deacon.** *Sterling E. Matthews, 60, Midlothian, Va.*

136 **Lead singer of a Yiddish folk group.** *Alby Kass, 89, California*

137 **Retired firefighter and old-school barber.** *Roger Eckart, 78, Indiana*

138 **Mentor to other Memphis artists.** *Daniel Spector, 68, Memphis*

139 **Maestro of a steel-pan band.** *Martin Douglas, 71, New York City*

140 **Sign-language interpreter.** *Mary Minervini, 91, Oak Lawn, Ill.*

141 **Loved to figure out how things worked.** *Salomon S. Podgursky, 84, Morristown, N.J.*

142 **Tailor known for his exacting work and strong opinions.** *Dale E. Thurman, 65, Lexington, Ky.*

143 **Jazz pianist and patriarch of a family of musicians.** *Ellis Marsalis, 85, New Orleans*

144 **Rocket engineer in the early days of supersonic flight.** *Richard Passman, 94, Silver Spring, Md.*

145 **Champion of African-American art.** *David Driskell, 88, Hyattsville, Md.*

146 **Master of jazz guitar.** *Bucky Pizzarelli, 94, Saddle River, N.J.*

147 **Belfast-born fighter for L.B.G.T. and disability rights.** *Tarlach MacNiallais, 57, New York City*

148 **Social worker.** *Antonio Checo, 67, New York City*

149 **Fire chief who answered the call on 9/11.** *Albert Petrocelli, 73, New York City*

150 **Songwriter for rock, film and the stage.** *Adam Schlesinger, 52, Poughkeepsie, N.Y.*

151 **Liked the mental challenges of business.** *Frederick Brown Starr, 87, Greensboro, N.C.*

152 **Authority on aviation.** *Douglas Alan Roberts, 69, Vancouver, Wash.*

153 **Taught her girls sheepshead and canasta.** *Muriel M. Going, 92, Cedarburg, Wis.*

154 **Longtime registered nurse and hospital volunteer.** *Beverly Collins, 83, Portland, Maine*

155 **Worked as an engineer with Comcast.** *Scott Melter, 60, Wyoming, Minn.*

156 **One-man army.** *Florencio Almazo Morán, 65, New York City*

157 **Broadway costume dresser.** *Jennifer Robin Arnold, 67, New York City*

158 **Coach and Scout leader.** *John Nakawatase, 62, Lincolnwood, Ill.*

159 **Famous in family circles for his birria beef stew.** *Jesus Roman Melendez, 49, New York*

160 **"we called him the Grand Poobah."** *Ralph Plaisance, 87, Massapequa, N.Y.*

161 **Sang gospel music as a member of the Malone Sisters.** *Audrey Malone, 68, Chicago*

162 **Original member of the Navy's elite Underwater Demolition Team.** *Harold L. Hayes, 96, Fort Wright, Ky.*

163 **Father figure.** *Terrence George Driscoll, 87, Plymouth, Mich.*

164 **Always wanted to be near the ocean.** *Ronnie Estes, 73, Stevensville, Md.*

165 **Marketing expert who brought exotic foods to green grocers.** *Anita Fial, 87, New York City*

166 **Actress who wrote biographies of famous friends.** *Patricia Bosworth, 86, New York City*

167 **Two-time cancer survivor.** *Azade Kilic, 69, New York*

168 **Honored to march with the American Legion in many parades.** *John E. Broadly, 84, Scituate, Mass.*

169 **Taught math, English and history for over thirty years.** *Julia Maye Alexander, 81, Upland, Calif.*

170 **Found his special place at Big Bowman Pond.** *Bruce W. Sowalski, 68, Sand Lake, N.Y.*

171 **Congregation's founding member.** *Samuel Kramer, 91, Potomac, Md.*

172 **Pharmacy manager with young daughters.** *Sean Boynes, 46, Annapolis, Md.*

173 **True community activist.** *Nancy Ferguson, 77, Chicago*

174 **Police officer who was never at a loss for words.** *Marco DiFranco, 50, Chicago*

175 **Mom to six sons.** *Nonna Hoza, 101, Wilmette, Ill.*

176 **Dubbed the "pistol-packing preacher."** *Lucius Hall, 87, Chicago*

177 **Town councilman.** *Glenn Daniel Bellitto, 62, New York*

178 **All-around supporter of the Washington Huskies.** *Helen Molina, 85, Washington*

179 **Noted voiceover artist for radio and TV.** *Judith Plotkin-Goldberg, 88, Massachusetts*

180 **Entrepreneur and adventurer.** *Coby Adolph, 44, Chicago*

181 **Loved creating perfect smiles.** *Steven J. Huber, 64, Jefferson City, Mo.*

182 **Sports fan who loved Purdue University.** *Don Whan, 67, Indiana*

183 **Executive behind New York Philharmonic's economic growth.** *Albert K. Webster, 82, New York City*

184 **Joined Goldman Sachs in 1975.** *Kevin Masterson, 74, New York City*

185 **Survived being shot in the line of duty in 1984.** *Randy G. Addison, 64, Carrollton, Ga.*

186 **Proud to have logged over five million miles behind the wheel.** *Ronald Willenkamp, 75, Wisconsin*

187 **Expert marksman and firearms instructor.** *Robert Lee Amos, 66, Columbus, Ind.*

188 **Inveterate harmonica player.** *Lloyd Paul Leftwich, 91, Louisiana*

189 **Helped countless people by providing housing and support.** *Ronald Burdette Culp, 84, Redding, Calif.*

190 **Shared his produce with food pantries and his neighbors.** *Norman Walker Jr., 80, China Township, Mich.*

191 **Former aerospace engineering professor at Howard University.** *Peter Bainum, 82, Bethesda, Md.*

192 **Worker at O'Hare International Airport.** *Viraf Darukhanawalla, 77, Hoffman Estates, Ill.*

193 **Part of a tightknit family.** *Lula Fitzpatrick, 85, Dolton, Ill.*

194 **Retired therapist and mentor.** *Charles Miles, 72, Chatham, Ill.*

195 **Leader in integrating schools.** *Ann Kolb, 78, New York City*

196 **Known for her Greek chicken and stuffed peppers.** *Helen Kafkis, 91, Chicago*

197 **True outdoorsman.** *John A. Bailargeon, 72, Dennisport, Mass.*

198   Proud Union Ironworker of Local 7 for forty-five years. *Chester Dwulet, 68, Burlington, Mass.*

199   Stalwart church gospel singer. *Regina Dix-Parsons, 75, Schenectady, N.Y.*

200   Trustee for the Retired Detroit Police and Firefighters Association. *John Timothy Barr, 76, Rochester Hills, Mich.*

201   Veterinarian who served Harlem. *Julie Butler, 62, New York City*

202   Always seemed to be busy with some home project. *Antonio Nieves, 73, Chicago*

203   Met Opera violist and youth orchestra conductor. *Vincent Lionti, 60, New York City*

204   Had a passion for social justice. *Ann Youngerman Smoler, 87, New York City*

205   Armed the affordable housing movement with data and analysis. *Thomas Waters, 56, New York City*

206   His relentless passion was for his family and friends. *Luke Workoff, 33, Huntington, N.Y.*

207   Served with the Palm Beach County Sheriff's Office for fourteen years. *José Díaz-Ayala, 38, Palm Beach, Fla.*

208   Was helping to raise some of her dozen grandchildren. *Lakisha Willis White, 45, Orlando, Fla.*

209   Received numerous awards for her accounting skills. *Jeanne Hammond Byrnes, 97, Danbury, Conn.*

210   In the first class of girls admitted to the Bronx High School of Science. *Alice Coopersmith Furst, 87, Kentfield, Calif.*

211   Seahawks season-ticket holder. *Bobby Lee Barber, 84, Buckley, Wash.*

212   Especially proud of his Lithuanian heritage. *Thomas A. Adamavich, 78, Sheboygan, Wis.*

213   Volunteered for pet rescue organizations. *Kyra Swartz, 33, New York*

214   First in her family to graduate college. *Rhoda Hatch, 73, Chicago*

215   First black woman to graduate from Harvard Law School. *Lila A. Fenwick, 87, New York City*

216   Family jokester. *John Cassano, 70, Palos Park, Ill.*

217   Loved automobiles, especially trucks. *Eugene Lamar Limbrick, 41, Colorado Springs*

218   No one made creamed potatoes or fried sweet corn the way she did. *June Beverly Hill, 85, Sacramento*

219   Writer who inspired her Brooklyn high school students. *Kimarlee Nguyen, 33, Everett, Mass.*

220   Hotel banquet worker and Bangladeshi leader. *Kamal Ahmed, 69, New York City*

221   Sanitation worker living his fullest days. *Raymond Copeland, 46, New York City*

222   New father. *Israel Sauz, 22, Broken Arrow, Okla.*

223   Worked for over six decades in the wine and liquor industry. *Lester Eber, 82, New York*

224   Loved the ocean and enjoyed swimming and boating. *Harry P. Misthos, 87, San Francisco Bay Area, Calif.*

225   Preferred bolo ties to neckties, suspenders to belts. *Leo Sreebny, 98, Seattle*

226   Could fix almost anything. *Robert Barghaan, 88, New York City*

227   Sang in her church choir for forty-two years. *Patricia H. Thatcher, 79, Clifton Park, N.Y.*

228   Strong advocate for health care policy. *Howard Alexander Nelson Jr., 84, New Orleans*

229   Loved the Jersey Shore music scene. *Allan Joseph Dickson Jr., 67, New Jersey*

230   She was known to many as Babs. *Barbara Yazbeck Vethacke, 74, St. Clair Shores, Mich.*

231   Always busy looking out for others. *Timothy Branscomb, 32, Chicago*

232   Known as "Big Wolf" to the basketball players he coached. *Jim J. Wolf Sr., 72, South Holland, Ill.*

233   Widely surmised he could have played Major League Baseball. *Paul Warech, 86, Vineland, N.J.*

234   Candy striper at St. Raphael's Hospital. *Antoinette Marie Lutz, 91, Chester, Conn.*

235   Owned Frainee Water Trucks for forty-four years. *Vincent G. Frainee, 68, Redlands, Calif.*

236   A heart of service. *Andrew Kowalczyk, 63, Coral Gables, Fla.*

237   Social worker who dedicated her life to others. *Jana Prince, 43, Gretna, La.*

238   Fourth-generation owner of Mario's restaurant, a Bronx institution. *Joseph Migliucci, 81, White Plains, N.Y.*

239   Founded Strategy Associates. *Reuben Gutoff, 92, New York City*

240   Retired New York Supreme Court justice. *Gerard Rosenberg, 85, New York City*

241   Loved to referee basketball games. *Marty Derer, 56, New Jersey*

242   Took furniture repair to the level of an art form. *Harold Reisner, 78, Pittsburgh*

243   Well known in the world of agility dog training. *Clark Osojnicki, 56, Stillwater, Minn.*

244   Directed Alba House Cornerstone Bookstore in lower Manhattan. *Kevin John Cahill, 83, New York City*

245   Known for having a smile on her face. *Janissa Delacruz, 31, Haverstraw, N.Y.*

246   Member for over forty-six years of the Operating Engineers Union, Local No. 106. *Clifford J. Williams, 81, Schaghticoke, N.Y.*

247   Unwavering faith and dedication to the Catholic Church. *Elizabeth Batista, 57, Waterbury, Conn.*

248   Nicknamed "Boxcar Bob" for his luck in shaking dice. *Robert L. Crahen, 87, Waunakee, Wis.*

249   Worked in construction and served in the Army. *Robert LeBlanc, 87, Cambridge, Mass.*

250   Chicago firefighter. *Mario Araujo, 49, Chicago*

251   People were her hobby. *Mari Jo Davitto, 82, Thornton, Ill.*

252   Gentle giant, athlete and musician. *Torrin Jamal Howard, 26, Waterbury, Conn.*

253   Volunteered his time to church car raffles, fund-raisers and picnics. *James V. Walsh, 78, New Jersey*

254   Immigrated to New York from a German refugee camp after World War II. *Liudas Karolis Mikalonis, 86, Berkley, Mich.*

255   Fierce advocate for educational opportunity. *Gene Zahas, 78, Oakland, Calif.*

256   Thought it was important to know a person's life story. *William D. Greeke, 55, Massachusetts*

257   Her size belied her strength and spirit. *Beatrice Rubin, 96, New Jersey*

258   Lived in the house he grew up in. *Jack Butler, 78, Indiana*

259   Took great joy in writing little ditties under her pen name, Penelope Penwiper. *Susan Grey Hopp Crofoot, 97, Westwood, N.J.*

260   Spent some of his happiest hours hiking in the Adirondacks. *James David Gewirtzman, 72, New City, N.Y.*

261   Endlessly curious, never really finished. *Morris Loeb, 90, Northbrook, Ill.*

262   Budding therapist with a gift for empathy. *Hailey Herrera, 25, New York City*

263   Leader of the Novominsker Hasidic dynasty. *Yaakov Perlow, 89, New York City*

264   Did two tours through the Panama Canal to Antarctica. *Joseph F. Kelly, 81, New York City*

265   Country-folk singer who was a favorite of Bob Dylan. *John Prine, 73, Nashville*

266   Quiet hero. *Perry Buchalter, 63, Florida*

267   Loved animals, had dogs and cats, and rode horses. *Monica Maley, 74, Rehoboth Beach, Del.*

268   Mentored by the computer science pioneer Grace Hopper. *Thomas Tarbell Russell, 83, Longmeadow, Mass.*

269   Backyard birds were known to eat from her hand. *Ruth Skapinok, 85, Roseville, Calif.*

270   Her favorite thing was meeting new people. *Faralyn Havir, 92, Minnesota*

271   Bus driver and school security guard. *Marlon Alston, 46, Chicago*

272   Pastor of Mt. Sinai Church of God in Christ. *James O'Brien Johnson, 74, Joplin, Mo.*

273   Stopped working to look after his aging parents. *Joseph W. Hammond, 64, Chicago*

274   Columbia University historian of U.S. presidents. *Henry F. Graff, 98, Greenwich, Conn.*

275   Worked mostly factory jobs to support his family. *Peter Kafleis, 91, Chicago*

276   Moved antiques for more than 25 years. *Tommie Adams, 71, Chicago*

277   Teacher's aide. *Johnnie D. Veasley, 76, Country Club Hills, Ill.*

278   More adept than many knew. *Myra Helen Robinson, 57, Detroit*

279   Professor at the Salter School. *Roger Mckinney-Wagner, 73, Lowell, Mass.*

280   Enjoyed talking sports with family. *Sean Christian Keville, 47, New Providence, N.J.*

281   One of the few African-American corporate bond traders on Wall Street. *John Herman Clomax, Jr., 62, Newark*

282   Restaurateur favored by salsa music's stars. *José Torres, 73, New York City*

283   Longtime dentist. *Conrad Duncker, 99, Chicago*

284   His greatest accomplishment was his relationship with his wife. *Dante Dennis Flagello, 62, Rome, Ga.*

285   Member of the Literacy Volunteers of America. *Mary M. Desole, 93, Poughkeepsie, N.Y.*

286 Face behind the counter at a family-owned grocery store. *Vera Flint, 97, Beverly, Mass.*

287 First responder during the 9/11 attacks. *Mike Field, 59, Valley Stream, N.Y.*

288 Social worker and then a political fundraiser. *Chianti Jackson Harpool, 51, Baltimore*

289 Sang her grandchildren a song on the first day of school each year. *Clara Louise Bennett, 91, Albany, Ga.*

290 Featured in multiple Broadway productions. *Ilona Murai Kerman, 96, New York*

291 Brooklyn cabbie who found a home in Buddhism. *Stuart Cohen, 73, New York City*

292 Called "The Captain" by friends and family. *George J. Foerst Jr., 99, New Jersey*

293 Wanted everyone to feel welcome. *Mauricio Valdivia, 52, Chicago*

294 Advocate for others with disabilities. *Robert Dugal, 58, Oak Park, Ill.*

295 Photographer, gourmet cook, sparkling hostess and traveler. *Sharyn Lynn Vogel, 74, Aurora, Colo.*

296 Helped drive the family car along Route 66. *Robert Charles Bazzell, 88, Novi, Mich.*

297 Deep-hearted country girl. *Claudia Obermiller, 73, Nebraska*

298 Republican freshman in the state Legislature. *Reggie Bagala, 54, Lockport, La.*

299 Man of faith and a proud Irish-American. *Richard Joseph Lenihan Jr., 55, Pearl River, N.Y.*

300 Made friends everywhere he went. *Deyrold Arteaga, 66, Central Valley, N.Y.*

301 Secretary to a New Jersey judge. *Estelle Kestenbaum, 91, Leonia, N.J.*

302 Opened a Los Angeles preschool. *Artemis Nazarian, 88, Englewood Cliffs, N.J.*

303 Freed from life in prison. *Myles Coker, 69, New York City*

304 Lifelong karate instructor. *Richard Alexander Ross Jr., 66, Boynton Beach, Fla.*

305 Made what she had work for her. *Helen Boles Days, 96, Wynnewood, Pa.*

306 He loved his wife and said, "Yes, dear" a lot. *Marcus Edward Cooper Jr., 83, Louisiana*

307 Veteran corrections officer and father of three. *Nelson Perdomo, 44, Middlesex County, N.J.*

308 Retired bank teller. *Rosemarie Amerosi, 87, New York City*

309 Worked for the Orange County Highway Department. *Timothy H. Gray, 66, Orleans, Ind.*

310 Security worker who died the same day as his wife. *Tommie Brown, 82, Gary, Ind.*

311 Died on the same day as her husband. *Doris Brown, 79, Gary, Ind.*

312 Never drew attention to herself. *Marie Scanlan Walker, 99, Louisiana*

313 Known as Big Momma to all who loved her. *Frances M. Pilot, 81, Wall, N.J.*

314 Loved writing birthday and holiday cards, poems and lists. *Denise Camille Buczek, 72, Bristol, Conn.*

315 Lifelong pacifist. *John B. Ahrens, 96, Newton, Mass.*

316 A decades-long career in ministry. *Parker Knoll, 68, Indiana*

317 Worked as a special education teacher for many years. *Kerri Ann Kennedy-Tompkins, 48, Garrison, N.Y.*

318 Former hairstylist and avid New York Yankees fan. *Rosemarie Franzese, 70, Nevada*

319 Math reader for Recordings for the Blind. *Bernard David Seckler, 95, Newton, Mass.*

320 Owner of Paris Blues, a beloved Harlem jazz joint. *Samuel Hargress Jr., 84, New York City*

321 Retired from Sears Outlet Stores as an assistant manager. *Michael Lee Jordan, 69, McLeansville, N.C.*

322 Nothing delighted him more than picking up the bill. *Merrick Dowson, 67, San Francisco Bay Area, Calif.*

323 Known for his knowledge of local history. *Wesley Richard Fahrbach II, 69, Fremont, Ohio*

324 Discovered his true calling when he started driving a school bus. *Harley E. Acker, 79, Troupsburg, N.Y.*

325 Caretaker of her neighborhood. *Arlola Rawls, 81, Chicago*

326 Brought smiles to everyone he interacted with. *Roger Liddell, 65, Flint, Mich.*

327 Inspiring math teacher. *Maclear Jacoby Jr., 93, Washington, D.C.*

328 Member of Harness Racing Hall of Fame. *Phil Langley, 83, Frankfort, Ill.*

329 Worked forty years for The New York Times. *Charles Constantino, 86, Menlo Park, N.J.*

330 Mathematician known as the "magical genius." *John Horton Conway, 82, New Brunswick, N.J.*

331 Developer and friend of the president. *Stanley Chera, 77, New York City*

332 Realtor and philanthropist who socialized with celebrities. *Robby Browne, 72, New York City*

333 Acting teacher and a founder of the American Place Theater. *Wynn Handman, 97, New York City*

334 Cartoonist and an expert on musicals. *Adam Kovacs, 72, New York City*

335 Manager of the S.W. Brown & Son Funeral Home. *Peter Brown, 53, New Jersey*

336 Great-grandmother with a flair for pizzelles. *Irene Gasior, 94, Pennsylvania*

337 Trombonist who once turned down an offer to join Duke Ellington's orchestra. *Stanley L. Morse, 88, Stark County, Ohio*

338 Had a mystic's direct sense of wonder and oneness. *Margaret Laughlin, 91, Massachusetts*

339 Retiree determined to spoil her granddaughter. *Cynthia Whiting, 66, La Plata, Md.*

340 I.T. manager with "an eye for beautiful and unusual things." *Steve Joltin, 75, Rockville, Md.*

341 Police officer turned pastor. *Gerald Glenn, 66, Richmond, Va.*

342 Excelled in the kitchen. *Doris Mae Burkhart Kale, 98, Pennsylvania*

343 Man who seemed to know everything. *Luther Coleman, 108, Evergreen Park, Ill.*

344 Stockbroker who founded Doherty Financial Services. *Ben Doherty, 83, Boston*

345 Loved to dance. *Josephine Posnanski, 98, New Jersey*

346 Collector of stamps and coins. *Alan A. Potanka, 68, Berlin, Conn.*

347 Left Peru and grabbed hold of the American dream. *Orlando Moncada, 56, Bronxville, N.Y.*

348 Graffiti artist with a generous spirit. *Fernando Miteff, 60, New York City*

349 Anywhere he went, he took pictures. *John Watson, 73, Philadelphia*

350 Editor at the Ladies' Home Journal. *Joyce Posson Winston, 93, North Bergen, N.J.*

351 Would walk her children to school every morning. *Maria Garcia-Rodelo, 52, Nevada*

352 Co-owned the Bark-and-All logging company. *Vinton Timely Mason, 86, Beaumont, Mich.*

353 Volunteer youth football coach. *John Schoffstall, 41, Terre Haute, Ind.*

354 Photographer of the Freedom Riders. *Theodore Gaffney, 92, Washington, D.C.*

355 Radio host and youth advocate. *Harold Davis Jr., 63, Chicago*

356 "Mayor of Martin Avenue." *Michael Giangrande Sr., 78, Bellmore, N.Y.*

357 Lifelong educator. *John B. Lynch, 76, Wilmington, Mass.*

358 A million dollar-smile. *Marvin L. Thomas, 81, Sun Lakes, Ariz.*

359 Worked more than thirty years for General Motors. *Timothy Ross, 68, Michigan*

360 Active in her church. *Sherrell Stokes, 54, Chicago*

361 Longtime high school referee. *Larry Jones, 61, Chicago*

362 Reader of books on birds and other wildlife. *Shirley S. D'Stefan, 90, Florham Park, N.J.*

363 Staff member and mentor at the Milwaukee Rescue Mission. *Billy Ross, 53, Milwaukee*

364 Known as the "fashionista" in her nursing home. *Helen Silvia, 96, Brockton, Mass.*

365 Worked at the Home Depot. *Davis Begaye, 48, Cudei, N.M.*

366 Daughter of Italian immigrants. *Rose Mary Infantino, 88, Rye Brook, N.Y.*

367 Animator for Disney films, including "The Little Mermaid." *Ann Sullivan, 91, Woodland Hills, Calif.*

368 Art supply businessman with a romantic streak. *Norman Gulamerian, 92, New Providence, N.J.*

369 Exceptional radiologist. *Kenneth L. Jewel, 78, Mountain Lakes, N.J.*

370 Last of the WWII Polish fighter pilots. *Jerzy Glowczewski, 97, New York City*

371 Built the family heating-oil business into a successful company. *Joan M. Heaney, 77, Upper Brookville, N.Y.*

372 Always put her children first. *Delia Regina DiTullio, 91, Jamaica Plain, Mass.*

373 Classy lady with style and elegance. *Jeanne Stone Rusnak, 84, Endicott, N.Y.*

374 Shared her knowledge and love of reading. *Anita Robinson, 94, Minnesota*

375 Enjoyed being a waterman on his work boat on Chesapeake Bay. *William U. Roulette III, 93, Stroudsburg, Pa.*

376 Trailblazing deputy sheriff. *Antoinette Meyer, 95, Crownsville, Md.*

377 Brought the family to church every week. *Michael Wrotniak Jr., 92, Glen Cove, N.Y.*

378 Pillar in the Detroit community. *Edmon C. Carmichael, 79, Detroit*

379   Alabama native who led travel agencies in Florida. *Carol Davis, 80, Manatee County, Fla.*

380   Former art teacher. *Tom Ferguson, 71, Chicago*

381   Babysitter for the local church. *Lela Reed, 95, Country Club Hills, Ill.*

382   Known for her amazing sense of humor. *Joan Cecile Berngen, 69, Burbank, Ill.*

383   Definition of love, loyalty, and the ability to serve others. *Gwendolyn A. Carmichael, 72, Detroit*

384   Known as the bonfire builder. *James Lowell Miller Jr., 64, Cedar Rapids, Iowa*

385   Her hobbies included reading, especially cookbooks. *Dolores A. Vail, 89, Torrington, Conn.*

386   Great mentor to many. *William Brett Tracy, 61, Snellville, Ga.*

387   Principal's assistant. *Ellen Spencer, 70, Newburgh, N.Y.*

388   Encyclopedia executive with perfect timing. *Stanley Moser, 88, Fort Lee, N.J.*

389   Home helper for many years. *Linda Nute, 61, Hazel Crest, Ill.*

390   Distinguished scholar. *William H. Gerdts, 91, New York City*

391   Dedicated her life to peace, diplomacy and human rights. *Ella King Russell Torrey, 94, Philadelphia*

392   Railroad worker with a big, joyful personality. *Michael Hill, 58, Glassboro, N.J.*

393   Boxing aficionado. *Richard Kiddle, 76, Beverly, Mass.*

394   Retail executive who led Selfridges. *Roy Northway Stephens, 85, New Canaan, Conn.*

395   Survivor who taught about the Holocaust. *Margit Buchhalter Feldman, 90, Somerset, N.J.*

396   Taught senior citizens computer and Internet skills. *Shidao Wang, 72, New York City*

397   Bravely fought a monthlong battle with Covid-19. *John Joseph Crowe, 56, Saint Johns, Fla.*

398   Accountant who achieved the American dream by founding a firm. *Sushil Kumar, 63, Roslyn Heights, N.Y.*

399   Trailblazing New Jersey nurse. *Corliss Henry, 95, Summit, N.J.*

400   While revelers did the "Soul Train" line at a wedding, he combined it with "The Worm." *Levie Barkley, 69, Chicago*

401   Restaurant owner. *Saul Moreno, 58, Chicago*

402   Volunteered for her parish, hand-making rosaries. *Manda Klancir, 90, Brookfield, Ill.*

403   Father figure to hundreds of young men. *Milton Sivels Jr., 68, Richton Park, Ill.*

404   Brakeman for the Chicago and Northwestern railroad. *Frank Miszkiewicz, 94, Aurora, Ill.*

405   Artist, photographer and mentor. *Philemon Najieb, 70, Chicago*

406   Worked on construction projects. *Albert H. Irwin, 86, Brownsville, Ore.*

407   Gained notoriety for his freeform dancing at family functions. *Philip A. Scardilli, 91, Colonia, N.J.*

408   Work was a big part of her life, and she derived much satisfaction from it. *Shirley Eileen Zimmerman, 92, Dearborn, Mich.*

409   First woman on her block to work outside the home. *Marlene B. Mandle, 88, Collingswood, N.J.*

410   Big guy with an even bigger heart. *Jeffrey Ronald Henry Muzljakovich, 56, Centerbook, Conn.*

411   The rock that held her family together. *Mary E. Mack, 84, Athens, Pa.*

412   Film professor and screenwriter. *Milena Jelinek, 84, New York City*

413   Inventive landscape photographer. *John Pfahl, 81, Buffalo*

414   Architect and Holocaust survivor. *Joseph Feingold, 97, New York City*

415   Saxophonist and master of "cool" jazz. *Lee Konitz, 92, New York City*

416   Survived by his wife of sixty-one years. *John Bradford Hubert II, 83, Beverly Hills, Mich.*

417   Always ready with a one-liner to lighten the mood. *Ken Caley, 59, San Clemente, Calif.*

418   Never let anyone mess with his younger brother. *Rodrick Samuels, 49, Orlando, Fla.*

419   Longtime member of the Quincy Republican City Committee. *Sandra McCauley, 83, Quincy, Mass.*

420   Worked as a secretary for Grumman Aerospace for nearly twenty-five years. *Ida Esposito, 92, Melville, N.Y.*

421   A twenty-five-year career at IBM. *Charles Robert Keal, 84, Maple Grove, Minn.*

422   Many appreciated his straight talk. *Jerome Michael Zottolo, 75, San Diego*

423   His "all in the pot" cookies will remain a family tradition. *Benjamin DiGiovanni, 90, New York City*

424   Loved to read and play bingo. *Nancy M. Allen, 91, New York City*

425   Longshoreman for New York piers. *Onielo De Luzio, 90, New York City*

426   Nursing assistant at the center of an outbreak. *Lawrence Nokes, 69, Maryland*

427   Transport worker. *Michael Miller, 60, Clinton, Md.*

428   Jazz bassist who returned to music after thirty years. *Henry Grimes, 84, New York City*

429   Coached youth baseball. *Harold Dixon, 60, Egg Harbor Township, N.J.*

430   He deserved the title Coach. *Marcus Pino, Sr., 42, Alamo Chapter, N.M.*

431   Loved to don Groucho glasses and tell jokes. *Allen Joseph Spinner, 71, Streamwood, Ill.*

432   Delighted in educating thousands of children over three decades. *Elaine Cupka, 86, Potomac, Md.*

433   Sang at countless weddings. *James Kevin Malloy, 67, Oxford, Miss.*

434   Championed desegregation. *Robert Bruce Harrell, 90, Carbondale, Ill.*

435   Smithsonian music curator. *James Merle Weaver, 82, New York*

436   Great-great-grandmother. *Cathryn Wood, 94, Detroit*

437   His ever-morphing and repetitive stories will be missed. *Ronald Wilfred LePage, 81, Grand Rapids, Mich.*

438   Worked tirelessly as a mental health advocate. *Laurie Appell, 70, Hartford, Conn.*

439   Nurse with a love for language. *Verla L. Courey, 88, South Windsor, Conn.*

440   Quoted Longfellow and Tennyson from memory. *Alan F. Knupp, 83, Newton, Mass.*

441   Known to many for his amazing Donald Duck impersonation. *Stanley Marvin Grossman, 83, Nanuet, N.Y.*

442   Taught French and etymology for twenty-seven years. *Kim A. Replogle Blanchar, 68, Avon, Ind.*

443   Presented quilts annually at the East Cobb Quilting Guild Show. *Nola Kathleen LaBudde, 71, Smyrna, Ga.*

444   Soft-spoken and genuine. *Alex Ruperto, 52, Glen Ridge, N.J.*

445   Subway car inspector in Manhattan. *Ferdi German, 41, Poughkeepsie, N.Y.*

446   Spent her youth at foreign service postings. *Martha Leroy Wilson, 76, Arlington, Va.*

447   A long career as a pharmacist. *Thomas William Campbell, 87, Midlothian, Va.*

448   Would hold scientific discussions over dinner. *Ina Shaw Mirviss, 93, Stamford, Conn.*

449   Former Angolan freedom fighter. *Zoao Makumbi Sr., 75, Lanham, Md.*

450   Represented Delaware in senior bowling tournaments. *Owen Moreland Parks, 80, Milford, Del.*

451   Was never afraid to sing or dance. *Angeline Michalopulos, 92, Des Plaines, Ill.*

452   Survived the sinking of his troopship in the English Channel. *Robert R. Stout, 95, Dennis, Mass.*

453   Glue to the family. *Moses Jones, 83, Chicago*

454   Driving force in establishing L.S.U.-Eunice. *Veil David DeVillier, 85, Baton Rouge, La.*

455   Young, healthy guy who took care of himself. *Ronaldo Ferrari, 42, Berlin, Conn.*

456   There is not a Louis L'Amour Western he had not read three times. *Arthur Winthrop Barstow, 93, Hadley, Mass.*

457   Seminole Police Department officer. *Calvin Harrison, 78, Florida*

458   Medal of Honor winner for Vietnam War heroics. *Bennie G. Adkins, 86, Opelika, Ala.*

459   Uniter of Nigerians in New York. *Jonathan Adewumi, 57, Bayonne, N.J.*

460   Bakery owner attuned to the West Indies. *Conrad Ifill, 81, Hempstead, N.Y.*

461   Clarinetist who wanted music to be easily accessible. *Paul Shelden, 79, Hewlett, N.Y.*

462   Soprano of opera companies in New York and Hamburg. *Arlene Saunders, 89, New York City*

463   World War II veteran whose twin died in the Spanish Flu epidemic a century ago. *Philip Kahn, 100, Westbury, N.Y.*

464   Art historian of East Harlem, N.Y. *Mario César Romero, 78, New York City*

465   Stylish archaeologist and champion dachshund breeder. *Iris Love, 86, New York City*

466   Winner of the art prize at Mt. Holyoke. *Andrea Ruth Ludgin, 81, Oyster Bay, N.Y.*

467   Vice president at an insurance firm. *Jane Krumrine, 82, Merion Station, Pa.*

468   Former firefighter. *Charlie Hopper, 78, Augusta, Maine*

469   Secretary turned tax consultant. *Judith Lee Arkerson, 77, Dover, N.H.*

470   Played football for Terre Haute South. *Larry Sylvester Hutchinson Jr., 27, Terre Haute, Ind.*

471   Helped establish many credit unions. *Charles Donald Neal, Sr., 91, Broken Arrow, Okla.*

472   Optimist. *Bill Mantell, 68, East Meadow, N.Y.*

473 Voice of the Naval Academy football stadium for three decades. *William E. Jackman, 85, Reston, Va.*

474 Secretary for the chairman of the Joint Chiefs of Staff. *Ruth Hunter, 96, Washington, D.C.*

475 Lifetime member of the Ladies' Auxiliary, V.F.W. Post 9400. *Patricia Plante, 84, Peoria, Ariz.*

476 His name was engraved on the Stanley Cup. *Barry G. Fisher, 69, Old Brookville, N.Y.*

477 Family man, risk-taker, teaser and sports lover. *Paul J. Foley Jr., 77, Chicago*

478 Rose each morning at 5 a.m. to read the Bible. *John Larry Sartain, 77, Des Plaines, Ill.*

479 Owned and operated Carey's Supermarket for many years. *Carol Carey, 84, Cuthbert, Ga.*

480 Served in Belgium, France, and Germany during WWII. *Joseph J. Angi Sr., 95, New York*

481 Los Angeles sports fan. *Paul Martinez, 70, West Covina, Calif.*

482 Enjoyed taking walks through town. *Michael I. Sumergrad, 64, Mansfield, Ohio*

483 Enjoyed attending reunions with fellow sailors. *John F. Cannon, 89, Allentown, Pa.*

484 Well-regarded bailiff and mentor to colleagues. *Eric Frazier, 44, New Orleans*

485 Civic leader and mediating force. *Kenneth Saunders III, 43, Decatur, Ga.*

486 Worked for Radio Free Europe. *Justin Liuba, 95, Springfield, Mass.*

487 General surgeon who volunteered to treat Covid-19 patients. *Barry Webber, 67, New York City*

488 Exemplified the women of the Greatest Generation. *Gloria Zimmerman, 97, White Plains, N.Y.*

489 Sympathetic ear. *Ruthie Jacqueline Stephens Turner, 86, Alabama*

490 Stylish dancer who could lead or follow. *Gerry Ellis, 91, Philadelphia*

491 Authored a well-regarded biography of Sarah Tyson Rorer. *Emma Weigley, 87, Philadelphia*

492 Attended every weekend A's game, almost without exception. *Scott Douglas Woodard, 67, Oakland, Calif.*

493 Always chose to work with the most at-risk students. *Steven L. Freedman, 71, Syosset, N.Y.*

494 Loved art and making cards. *Carla Thompson, 67, Washington, D.C.*

495 Immigrated from Hong Kong. *Yuet Ming Wong, 91, Chicago*

496 Dedicated nurse. *Josephine Tapiru, 56, Chicago*

497 Ticket clerk who rose to lead the L.I.R.R. *Raymond Kenny, 68, Lindenhurst, N.Y.*

498 Husband lost two days before his wife of sixty-two years. *Thomas Neal Therrian, 84, Ellenton, Fla.*

499 Formidable professor, amiable pastor. *Herbert Nygren, 91, Carol Stream, Ill.*

500 Michigan's youngest victim of the coronavirus pandemic. *Skylar Herbert, 5, Detroit*

501 Survived by her husband of seventy years. *Nonna Jean Knight, 93, Des Moines*

502 Gifted pitcher who never made the big leagues. *Steve Dalkowski, 80, New Britain, Conn.*

503 Dispensed tough but empathetic love to her students. *Patricia McGowan, 80, New York City*

504 Patent lawyer who recovered a family painting looted by the Nazis. *David Toren, 94, New York City*

505 Combative councilman and judge. *Noach Dear, 66, New York City*

506 Modern-day renaissance woman. *Myrtha Celifie, 91, McHenry, Ill.*

507 Her sarcastic sense of humor always made everyone smile. *Alice Fraher-Mason, 91, Weymouth, Mass.*

508 Cancer survivor at eighty-eight-years-old. *Stephen J. Clinton, 94, Rockland, Mass.*

509 Taught elementary school for more than thirty years. *Kathleen Devon Domenick, 67, Devon, Pa.*

510 Loved playing tennis. *Roxana Griswold Foreman, 85, Richmond, Va.*

511 Stayed home to raise her children. *Audrey L. Ercha, 92, Beverly, Mass.*

512 Master electrician. *John Joseph Christiana Jr., 80, Hartford, Conn.*

513 Loved the grocery business. *John Fusco, 68, Rochester, N.Y.*

514 Teacher passionate about respecting people with different abilities. *Cynthia Jean Falle, 72, Troy, N.Y.*

515 Active member and leader of the Taconic Hiking Club. *Willard John Hoyt, 87, Schodack, N.Y.*

516 Therapist for military veterans. *Calvin Richardson Jr., 57, La Plata, Md.*

517 A zest for life. *Ethel R. Fonti, 77, Beverly, Mass.*

518 Enjoyed the theaters of New York. *Joseph M. Kissane, 89, New York City*

519 Faithful in corresponding through cards and handwritten notes. *Beverly J. Plessinger, 88, Wooster, Ohio*

520 Worked in maintenance for the public schools. *Ralph R. Loranger, 74, Farmington, Conn.*

521 Known for throwing an annual Fourth of July party. *Craig Franken, 61, Sioux Falls, S.D.*

522 Firefighter and part-time Santa. *Fred J. Felella Jr., 58, Sugar Grove, Ill.*

523 Co-owned and operated Atwood Television and Radio Service. *Thomas I. Atwood, 80, Bluffton, S.C.*

524 Her strength was a thing of wonder. *Linda L. Orendorff, 80, Hilliard, Ohio*

525 Hospitality came easy to her. *Florence Marks, 96, Lancaster, Pa.*

526 Notorious for receiving the most holding calls. *Boro Lalich, 68, Indianapolis*

527 Well-respected criminal defense attorney. *Richard Emnett Powers, 76, Detroit*

528 Cherished grandfather. *John Francis McClintock, 84, Farmington Hills, Mich.*

529 Always had a smile and a twinkle in her eye. *Vincie Teresa DeRose, 57, Arlington, Mass.*

530 Her gardens flourished. *Mary Ann Scata, 90, Wethersfield, Conn.*

531 Proud of her Italian heritage. *Dorothy Cembrano Jay, 92, East Windsor, Conn.*

532 Highly successful Avon representative. *Edith Costanzo, 93, Wethersfield, Conn.*

533 Roaring voice that filled lecture halls. *Dennis Peters, 82, Indiana*

534 Exceptional billiard player. *Gaetano Lombardo, 70, Rockland County, N.Y.*

535 Her zest for life will live on. *Marie A. Detrick, 88, Sayre, Pa.*

536 Worked for more than fortyu years at the U.S. Department of Education. *Stanley M. Cohen, 86, Chevy Chase, Md.*

537 Lifelong dedication to family. *Carol Freedman, 88, New Rochelle, N.Y.*

538 Popular figure in the Philadelphia wine and spirits community. *Ron Waxman, 88, Pennsylvania*

539 Taught himself to play the drums. *Charles Dow Long, 82, Tempe, Ariz.*

540 Professor of English and philosophy at Gloucester County College. *Henry Burk Sullivan, 90, Haddonfield, N.J.*

541 New Hampshire state legislator and Dover City councilman. *Paul R. McQuade, 88, Dover, N.H.*

542 Loved bird-watching, fishing, and listening to music. *Frederick Koerner, 86, Minnesota*

543 Spent countless hours coaching baseball in Bartlesville. *Malcolm C. Shaw Jr, 77, Bartlesville, Okla.*

544 Wife who outlived her husband by less than two days. *Judy Therrian, 80, Ellenton, Fla.*

545 Corporate leader and animal rescue advocate. *Herb Baum, 83, Florida*

546 Youngest of twenty-one siblings. *Sawarrelita Redmond, 52, Riverdale, Ill.*

547 "Adventurer and a charmer." *Peter Laker, 93, Chicago*

548 Taught at several Baltimore-area schools. *Barbara Ann Loreck, 90, Pikesville, Md.*

549 Known in English as "Grandpa Boom" and in Lithuanian as "Senelis." *Anthony V. Racka, 86, Farmington Hills, Mich.*

550 France was always first and foremost in her heart. *Suzanne Raynal Gijsbers, 93, Michigan*

551 A thirty-year career at the Gillette Company. *Kenneth Richard Coombs, 75, Methuen, Mass.*

552 Worked as a computer specialist for the Department of Agriculture. *Eric F. Anderson, 80, Southfield, Mich.*

553 Gardener who won the title of Pickle King. *Theodore Robert Zaterka, 89, South Windsor, Conn.*

554 Avid fly fisherman. *Richard J. Conway III, 64, Amston, Conn.*

555 Pastor who "preached with a lot of strength and voice and sweat." *David Ford, 59, DeWitt Township, Mich.*

556 Longtime educator who was also a police officer. *Willie Gene Whitaker, 85, Texas*

557 Emmy-nominated TV producer behind "Knight Rider" and "Magnum, P.I." *Joel Rogosin, 87, Los Angeles*

558 Worked as a carpenter for more than forty years. *William F. Latimer, 75, Maryland*

559 Lifetime resident of Lewiston. *Crystal LaBelle, 87, Lewiston, Idaho*

560 Former president of Stanford University. *Donald Kennedy, 88, Redwood City, Calif.*

561 Boxing gym owner and beloved trainer. *Francisco Mendez, 61, Jersey City, N.J.*

562 A long career in horticulture. *Antoinette Tosco, 77, Bridgewater, N.J.*

563 Prosecuted mobsters, drug dealers and corrupt politicians. *Phil Foglia, 69, New York City*

564 Brother of Senator Elizabeth Warren. *Donald Reed Herring, 86, Norman, Okla.*

565 Loved dancing, opera, art, British mysteries and animals of all kinds. *Billie Jean Michael Habennehl, 90, Manassas, Va.*

566 Raised five children. *Mary Therese Loughery, 89, Abington, Pa.*

567 Motivating "legend" in a southwest Philadelphia school. *Gloria Allen Moskowitz, 88, Ardmore, Pa.*

568 Inducted into the Aircraft Engine Hall of Fame. *Stephen J. Chamberlin Jr., 91, Worcester, Mass.*

569 Insurance salesman famous for his self-help books. *Barry Kaye, 91, Boca Raton, Fla.*

570 Nurse working night shifts in the ICU. *Patricia Gibbons, 76, Naples, Fla.*

571 Mother outlived by her newborn. *Wogene Debele, 43, Baltimore*

572 Political scientist and congressional scholar. *Richard F. Fenno Jr., 93, Rye, N.Y.*

573 Art director for the ABC television shows "Emergence," "Luke Cage" and "The Punisher." *Matteo De Cosmo, 52, New York*

574 Had been planning to retire in April. *Celia Yap-Banago, 69, Kansas City, Mo.*

575 Talented athlete who played football, baseball and basketball. *Peter P. DeLuise, 63, New Jersey*

576 A passion for slot machines. *Dalma Holloway Torres, 73, Uniondale, N.Y.*

577 Served in the U.S. Army. *Louis B. Bernstein, 92, Roseland, N.J.*

578 Always enjoyed a good discussion involving politics. *Retha Elizabeth Contri Sharp, 98, Iowa*

579 Owned and operated Big Bob's Pizzerias. *Robert Adam Burns, 85, Michigan*

580 Last of his generation for his sixty nieces and nephews. *Raymond Paul Janssen, 96, Dowagiac, Mich.*

581 Shining light and an uplifting presence. *Kerry Lehman, 62, Jackson, Mich.*

582 Loved his truck, Dorney Park, Disney World, model trains, and especially California cheeseburgers. *James W. Landis, 57, Krocksville, Pa.*

583 E.M.T. and former Marine who rushed to the World Trade Center on 9/11. *Idris Bey, 60, New York City*

584 Served in the U.S. Army in Iran and with the C.D.C. fighting cholera in the Philippines. *Paul Ronald Joseph, 87, Forest Hills, N.Y.*

585 Member of Bethlehem United Methodist Church. *Bette Allred Weatherly, 93, Pleasant Garden, N.C.*

586 Feisty, unique lady to the end. *Anna Sternik Warren, 100, Binghamton, N.Y.*

587 Widely respected tenor saxophone player. *Robert Barnes, 82, Philadelphia*

588 Enjoyed bingo, watching TV and spending time with her family. *Dawn M. Peryer, 61, Plattsburgh, N.Y.*

589 She and her husband were pioneers in industrial catering. *Alma M. Carney, 91, Florida*

590 Senior corrections police officer. *Maria Gibbs, 47, Burlington County, N.J.*

591 Cherished grandfather. *Robert C. Moen Sr., 83, Schenectady, N.Y.*

592 Would talk to anybody about anything. *Jerry Alford, 60, Tuscaloosa, Ala.*

593 Cheerful, upbeat, thankful person. *Paul Edward Herbst, 92, Vernon, Conn.*

594 Skilled cook. *Mark Schroeder, 54, New York*

595 Loved seeing the full moon rise over the ocean. *Norman Leslie Jenkins, 91, Hingham, Mass.*

596 Enjoyed gardening, fishing, hunting, playing pranks and spending time with family. *Celestino Padilla Sr., 82, Rochester, N.Y.*

597 Taught the fourth and fifth grades. *Virginia Alice Rauth, 85, Lakewood, N.J.*

598 Tried to make everyone around him laugh. *Jeffrey Stanley Lin, 70, Middletown, N.J.*

599 Nurse for more than thirty years. *Joyce Pacubas-Le Blanc, 53, Darien, Ill.*

600 Enjoyed gardening, decorating and cooking. *Lucille Dolores Romer, 80, New Jersey*

601 Taught junior high science and math and farmed full-time. *Gerald Ringdahl, 87, North Dakota*

602 A five-year minor league baseball career. *Ed Smrekar, 88, Pennsylvania*

603 Outspoken, loving, caring, and compassionate. *Rachel Walters, 68, Cudei, N.M.*

604 Served as interim pastor to churches during difficult transitions. *Allen Francis Tinkham, 91, Newington, Conn.*

605 Aspiring leader in the Navajo Nation. *Valentina Blackhorse, 28, Kayenta, Ariz.*

606 Rapper known for sharp wordplay. *Fred the Godson, 41, New York City*

607 Was thirteen during World War II when she and her family were incarcerated at Manzanar. *Lillian Kimura, 91, Albany, N.Y.*

608 Enjoyed the church's women's bowling league. *Carol A. Castle, 80, Weymouth, Mass.*

609 Educator who said, "I didn't teach a subject. I taught children." *Ethel Hamburger, 92, Elkins Park, Pa.*

610 Vermont shop owner. *William Harrison Goldman, 87, New Jersey*

611 Longtime soccer referee. *Ronald Clark, 70, Ballston Lake, N.Y.*

612 Enjoyed spending time with her family and reminiscing about her horses. *Audrey LeMaire Morvant, 76, Abbeville, La.*

613 Hunted and fished and cooked what he caught. *Charles Willis Alston, 74, Seaford, Del.*

614 Expert polygraph examiner. *John J. Valentine, 86, Long Branch, N.J.*

615 Will be remembered for her spirit of adventure and wanderlust. *Marcia Rushford, 80, Alexandria, Va.*

616 Former merchant marine from Cape Verde. *Anibal Francisco de Brito, 90, Philadelphia*

617 Social butterfly. *Elizabeth Tevenan, 82, Brewster, Mass.*

618 Loved art, music, and animals. *Joan M. Cargill, 81, New Brunswick, N.J.*

619 Served in the Korean War and the Berlin airlift. *Kenneth K. Skoog, 90, Fargo, N.D.*

620 Worked as a maintenance man for J.M. Smucker for twenty-five years. *Quentin Cornell, 84, Orrville, Ohio*

621 Collector and talented artist. *Carl Robert Bentley, 78, Glastonbury, Conn.*

622 Enjoyed dancing, shooting pool and going to Soundview Beach. *Ronald Boccacio, 80, Hartford, Conn.*

623 Never seemed to know a stranger. *Clyde Addison Reichelderfer, 86, Ohio*

624 Had an exceptional recollection of local history. *Betty Jean Ringle, 87, Idaho*

625 Founder of PBS. *Gerald Slater, 86, Washington, D.C.*

626 Kept a scrapbook of the places he saw. *Walter M. Eagles Jr., 95, Fort Washington, Pa.*

627 Generous, blunt, and forever centered on her family. *Oluwayemisi Ogunnubi, 59, Chicago*

628 Remained proud of her Greek heritage. *Helen Demetoglous, 96, New Jersey*

629 Organized his Class of 1943 high school reunions through the 70th in 2013. *Calvin Tompkins Lucy Jr., 93, Virginia*

630 Enjoyed a thirty-seven-year career with the Rockville Centre Police Department. *John McKeon, 68, Islip, N.Y.*

631 High school library aide and a teacher's aide. *Margaret Skaliotis, 92, Boston*

632 If you asked her to do something, she did it. *Marion Klein, 87, St. Louis Park, Minn.*

633 Always the first to offer help to those in need. *Latasha Andrews, 33, New Jersey*

634 Avid reader and book club member. *Dorothy Alma Ennis D'Ostilio, 95, Fairfield, Conn.*

635 Buffalo front-line hospital worker. *John Poleon, 63, Erie County, N.Y.*

636 Involved in the early days of aerobic exercise. *Rona Iris Gertz, 74, New Jersey*

637 She helped immigrants and refugees get on their feet. *Patricia Rowe, 94, Buffalo*

638 Made his living from police work. *Joseph T. Cappello, 55, Melrose Park, Ill.*

639 Created her own version of "meals on wheels" for those in need. *Barbara Stack, 76, Perth Amboy, N.J.*

640 Faithfully served his country with the Air Force. *Robert Michael Sedor, 77, Hillsborough, N.J.*

641 Never knew anything but work. *Terry G. Thompson, 75, Indiana*

642 Her passion was geriatric care. *Brenda Lee Orebaugh, 62, Dayton, Va.*

643 Put himself through college. *Jorge F. Casals, 75, Manchester, Conn.*

644 Owned her own small businesses. *Lucille Marie Resto, 77, Rocky Hill, Conn.*

645 Performed in renowned venues such as Madison Square Garden. *Luis A. Frias, 65, Las Vegas*

646 Accomplished artist. *Pierina D. Borsoi, 90, Bethlehem, Pa.*

647 Scientist who explained the physics of sports. *Peter J. Brancazio, 81, Manhasset, N.Y.*

648 Haitian immigrant with a big heart. *Edith Richemond, 88, New York City*

649 Collector of dictionaries and lover of words. *Madeline Kripke, 76, New York City*

650 Spent his working years in the insurance industry. *Raphael Kaminer, 86, New York City*

651 Loving father. *Richard J. Rome, 91, Roslindale, Mass.*

652 Actively involved in the United Methodist Women. *Barbara J. Norris, 90, Weymouth, Mass.*

653 One of the first women of her generation to drive a car. *Eve Rudin, 103, Philadelphia*

654 His greatest accomplishment was serving as an ordained deacon. *Raymond W. Wilkinson Sr., 91, Weatherly, Pa.*

655 Only things he was more proud of than his military service were his children. *Bruce P. Biesenbach Sr., 74, Albany, N.Y.*

656 Loved karaoke, dancing, singing and playing bingo. *Louise N. Walsh, 71, Massachusetts*

657 Her will was indomitable. *Nora Malis, 97, Salem, N.H.*

658 Worked at Goodwill for more than twenty-five years. *Michael Albert Shubak, 60, Coraopolis, Pa.*

659 Studio musician in the late sixties in New York City. *Ron Frangipane, 75, Tinton Falls, N.J.*

660 Awarded the Combat Infantryman Badge, Purple Heart, and Bronze Star. *Richard M. Glidden, 95, Orleans, Mass.*

661 Enlisted in the Women's Army Corps on her twenty-first birthday in 1944. *Britta Lou Miller, 97, Ohio*

662 Enjoyed family dinners and celebrations. *Ellen Elizabeth Fabry, 70, Burlington, N.J.*

663 Quiet and humble member of a prayer circle. *Mary Gilbert, 84, Mansfield, Mass.*

664 Lifelong teacher with a master's degree in special education. *Martha Eddy O'Brien, 86, Hartford, Conn.*

665 Started his own business. *Henry N. Dubois, 84, East Hartford, Conn.*

666 Loved to watch old Western movies. *Joseph Colasurdo, 85, Jersey City, N.J.*

667 His family was the most important accomplishment of his life. *Edward A. Masterson, 56, Yonkers, N.Y.*

668 Award-winning journalist, author and community activist. *Robert C. Samuels, 83, New York*

669 Dearly loved Kentucky. *Lillian Press, 95, Kentucky*

670 Outlet to talk about everything and anything. *Rosemarie Theresa Torrance, 60, Wilmington, Del.*

671 Enjoyed gardening, camping and making people laugh. *Clarence Robert Ellis, 93, Rochester, N.Y.*

672 Member of the Bell retirees. *Mary Frances Parsels Dennis, 82, Mechanicsville, Va.*

673 Had a knack for games of chance. *Richard Daniel Harris, 86, Danvers, Mass.*

674 Major college donor in Florida. *Carole Kaye, 87, Boca Raton, Fla.*

675 Swam over one mile each week. *Eva Charlotte Julewitz, 91, Woonsocket, R.I.*

676 Loved old Western movies, Elvis's music and the Dallas Cowboys. *Tony Maldonado, 66, Waxahachie, Texas*

677 Worked for the F.A.A. as a flight operations safety officer, retiring at eighty-five. *Ross L. Saddlemire, 87, Port Jefferson, N.Y.*

678 Had a vision to provide sophisticated medical care to rural areas. *John Robert Oglesbee, 80, Tahlequah, Okla.*

679 City planner and longtime community volunteer. *Norton A. Kent, 96, Gwynedd, Pa.*

680 Avid reader and knitter. *Karen Kay Bentley, 79, Sturgeon Bay, Wis.*

681 Surgical technologist. *Juan Martinez, 60, Chicago*

682 He could spit a watermelon seed halfway across a double lot. *Kenneth James Godwin, 94, Michigan*

683 Pastor at Navajo Baptist Temple. *Jimmy Walters, 71, Cudei, N.M.*

684 Rose to leadership of the Republican Party of Iowa. *Linda Joy Nassif, 76, Iowa*

685 Staff member at Trinity Elementary School in New Rochelle. *Emmy Falta, 41, New York*

686 Computer engineer at Pratt and Whitney for many years. *Anthony J. Valdati Jr., 83, Glastonbury, Conn.*

687 Worked for more than two decades as a social worker. *Catherine Drouin, 69, Methuen, Mass.*

688 Selected by the F.B.I. as a top recruit. *Irene Ann Allen, 80, Simsbury, Conn.*

689 Volunteered as a firehouse cook for over fifty years. *Hilda R. Nagel, 99, Whitehall, Pa.*

690 Worked for over thirty-three years at Westinghouse. *William G. Bennett, 84, Waverly, N.Y.*

691 Master jeweler and goldsmith. *Fritz Wilhelm Reisgies, 87, Alpine, N.J.*

692 Fought against the Covid-19 pandemic to save patients. *James Mahoney, 62, New York City*

693 In the Pennsylvania Voter Hall of Fame for voting in every November election for fifty years. *Wayne L. Wolford, 95, Pennsylvania*

694 Portrait oil and landscape watercolor painter. *Joan M. Hackney, 91, West Chester, Pa.*

695 Grammy-nominated gospel singer and record label founder. *Troy Sneed, 52, Jacksonville, Fla.*

696 Always the first one out on the dance floor. *Leslie Kalmus, 57, New Jersey*

697 Master storyteller, with a quick wit and a flair for the dramatic. *Ronald Jacobus, 81, Galloway, N.J.*

698 Had a love of everything automotive. *Russell Aucott, 71, Linwood, N.J.*

699 A fifty-six-year career as a produce manager at Stop and Shop. *Robert N. Winsor, 78, Marblehead, Mass.*

700 He was a master of all tools. *Daniel James Callahan, 90, Massachusetts*

701 Known for her strength and devotion to family. *Carole Montalbano, 83, Springfield, Ill.*

702 Former students will remember his brush cut and dry humor. *Alexander Webster Cruden Jr., 87, New York*

703 Accomplished quilter, calligrapher, and gardener. *Ann Bonville Trombly, 88, New York*

704 Loved jeeping, camping, barbecuing, building, and socializing. *Gary Tillery, 66, Tulare, Calif.*

705 Inspirational basketball coach. *Terrance Burke, 54, Maryland*

706 Ground mechanic for TWA. *Robert C. Blades, 84, Groveland, Mass.*

707 Shared a special bond with both of her sons. *Dorothy Murphy, 83, Salem, Mass.*

708 Proud of recently being promoted to Grampy. *Conrad Warren Buckley, 52, Clermont, Fla.*

709 Army veteran, business owner, free spirit and kvetch. *Daniel S. Pincu, 80, Asheville, N.C.*

710 Excellent cook, though she hated the task. *Asela E. Gejo, 92, New Jersey*

711 Celebrated Hartford Public High School basketball player. *Charles Jernigan, 61, Hartford, Conn.*

712 Core member of her congregation. *Dorthe J. Flick, 97, Clinton, Iowa*

713 Enjoyed entertaining his family by playing guitar and mandolin. *Peter Crisanti, 84, West Haven, Conn.*

714 Endeared himself to his nephews. *Joseph J. Ingram Jr., 66, New Britain, Conn.*

715 Enjoyed novels, crossword puzzles, art, and TV shows. *Yvonne S. Orlando, 81, Bethlehem, Pa.*

716 Renegade nun who ran a nonprofit anchor in Brooklyn. *Georgianna Glose, 73, New York City*

717 Fashionista. *Jean Adele Walkins, 92, Whitman, Mass.*

718 Worked at American Tobacco for thirty-one years. *Barbara Mae Barham, 88, Richmond, Va.*

719 Former A's minor-leaguer. *Miguel Marte, 30, New Jersey*

720 Enjoyed golfing. *Earl Avers, 92, Oregon, Ohio*

721 Retired from H&W Motor Express after thirty years. *John Pearson Brucher, 81, Cedar Rapids, Iowa*

722 Her greatest joy was spending time with her family. *Virginia Bettencourt, 92, Peabody, Mass.*

723 Highly respected by those who worked with him. *Michael L. Trombley, 79, West Brattleboro, Vt.*

724 Professional land surveyor and civil engineer. *Paul Nathan Fontenot, 80, Lafayette, La.*

725 Trained and accomplished singer. *Barbara Helen Richardson, 97, Bristol, Conn.*

726 Non-judgmental and empathetic listener. *Daniel James Parr, 60, Cape Cod, Mass.*

727 Nigerian immigrant studying to become a nurse. *Ijeoma Afuke, 35, Chicago*

728 Often the one to pick out birthday cakes for his children. *Isaias Mendoza, 63, Evanston, Ill.*

729 Enjoyed long drives, late nights and huge meals. *Jerome Berrien, 64, Chicago*

730 Go-to person for everybody. *Floyd Bluntson, 66, Chicago*

731 Voted "most debonair" in her high school yearbook. *Edie Morello, 97, Barrington, Ill.*

732 Strong-willed enough to keep her family in line. *Edith Gallo, 94, Palos Heights, Ill.*

733 Avid, lifelong trap shooter. *Paul Francis Siefert Sr., 77, Colerain Township, Ohio*

734 Traced her roots back over ten generations. *Dorothy May Thompson, 105, Des Moines*

735 Would stay awake on the night shift because she didn't want anyone to die alone. *Margaret Busha, 89, Mystic, Conn.*

736 Enjoyed international, square, and round dancing. *Frederick Anthony Palazzo, 87, Woburn, Mass.*

737 Worked at the Memorial Hospital of Rhode Island for twenty-three years. *Suchendra Singh, 43, Pawtucket, R.I.*

738 Huge Elvis fan. *Carmen Lydia Muniz Rodriguez, 76, Glastonbury, Conn.*

739 Ran Brownstone Amusements Carnival with her husband. *Elsie Rossitto, 92, Portland, Conn.*

740 Decorated Vietnam War veteran and member of the Seminole Tribe. *Don Osceola, 77, Hollywood, Fla.*

741 Mainstay of the Valhalla School District. *Nicholas Modugno, 91, New York*

742   Served in the Army Air Corps as an aviation electrician. *Charles Walter Calhoun, 93, Alexander City, Ala.*

743   Enjoyed planting perennial flower beds. *Marie Virginia Leto, 92, Kennett Square, Pa.*

744   Self-taught legal wiz. *Thomas Cotton, 54, Philadelphia*

745   Served in the Marine Corps from 1958 to 1961. *James E. Mann Jr., 86, Richmond, Va.*

746   Church choir director, soloist and organist. *Alice Louise Trout, 81, Pendleton, Ind.*

747   Loved his whole family. *Arthur Louis Thibault, 75, Andover, Mass.*

748   Author of children's stories. *Helen Wall, 91, Lawrence, Mass.*

749   Owned one of the first Spanish bodegas in the city of Lawrence. *Mercedes Santiago, 82, Lawrence, Mass.*

750   Visited many countries. *Dean Leroy Drake, 79, Chandler, Ariz.*

751   Helped friends and neighbors train their dogs. *Edward Russell Helfrich, 72, West Keansburg, N.J.*

752   Huge fan of Waynedale High School sports. *Calvin E. Messner, 77, Wooster, Ohio*

753   Hobbies included sewing, knitting, crafts, puzzles, painting, golf, bowling, and euchre. *Janet M. Brown, 91, Greece, N.Y.*

754   Authored the book "Making It In Radio." *Daniel Blume, 89, West Hartford, Conn.*

755   Enjoyed traveling throughout New England. *Jean Munson, 92, Plainville, Conn.*

756   Helped form an advocacy group for Latino families. *Jose Vitelio Gregorio, 61, New City, N.Y.*

757   Emergency worker in the Seminole Tribe. *Donald DiPetrillo, 70, Florida*

758   Writer who captured the Chinese experience abroad. *Yu Lihua, 90, Gaithersburg, Md.*

759   Professor at New York University Medical School. *Charles Goodstein, 82, Tenafly, N.J.*

760   Knew how to make an entrance. *Melita Baker, 89, Irvington, N.Y.*

761   Intelligent and industrious. *Joraine Sieber Groat, 97, Ann Arbor, Mich.*

762   Perfectionist and an excellent cook. *Nancy Reid, 97, Topsfield, Mass.*

763   Police detective who was once a firefighter. *Randall Clayton French, 39, Troy, N.Y.*

764   Paramedic who drove to New York to help fight the virus. *Paul Cary, 66, New York City*

765   Psychiatrist specializing in substance abuse. *Alyce Gullattee, 91, Washington, D.C.*

766   One of the first in Massachusetts to compete in the Special Olympics. *Emmanuel Demetri, 61, Gloucester, Mass.*

767   Gentle soul who appreciated the simple things in life. *Robert Steven Seldin, 62, Toms River, N.J.*

768   Bowled for over fifty years in various leagues. *Corinne Rhodes, 93, Oxford, Pa.*

769   Had a passion for soul food, cooking, music and her church. *Adrienne Eugina Doolin Howard, 75, Cedar Rapids, Iowa*

770   His love of wildlife and the marshes fueled his soul. *Stewart Markham Fish, 58, Hingham, Mass.*

771   Often at the farm tending to his flock and managing his inventory of acquired wonders. *Thomas Allen Catron, 65, Adel, Iowa*

772   Was pursuing a degree in history and anthropology. *Jonathan Crachat Carreira Ferreira, 26, Newington, Conn.*

773   Served as a Eucharistic minister and lector. *Anna Marie Lopiccolo, 74, Bristol, Conn.*

774   Enjoyed her friends and listening to music. *Julia Martinez, 62, Lubbock, Texas*

775   Beloved mother, grandmother, great-grandmother, and great-great-grandmother. *Betty Sue Harber Carney, 81, Grapevine, Texas*

776   Served on the Manhattan Project. *Arthur Rogers, 93, Mooresville, N.C.*

777   Beloved Westchester deputy fire chief. *Edward Ciocca, 62, White Plains, N.Y.*

778   Lifelong political radical. *David Bernstein, 78, New York City*

779   Employee of the Pilgrim's Pride poultry processing plant. *Adelfo Ruiz Calvo, 65, Sanford, N.C.*

780   Enjoyed winters in Florida and traveling with the Aircraft Campmates. *Helen Sutton, 93, Rocky Hill, Conn.*

781   Worked long, hard hours and still made time for everyone. *Wee Chu Wong, 90, Worcester, Pa.*

782   Would give up the shirt on his back if you needed it. *David E. Carman, 89, Egg Harbor Township, N.J.*

783   Educator who taught many offspring of her former students. *Marjorie L. Goolsby, 89, Marblehead, Mass.*

784   Child of San Francisco who walked across the Golden Gate Bridge on opening day. *Jean Marie Hazelwood, 93, San Mateo, Calif.*

785   Spent her last working days helping those who had the virus. *Sheena Renee Comfort Miles, 60, Morton, Miss.*

786   Advocate for gender, racial and L.G.B.T. equality. *Ruth E. Shinn, 97, Washington, D.C.*

787   Loved classical and choral music. *Elizabeth Harris Tirrell, 95, Hillsborough, N.J.*

788   Enjoyed antiquing with her daughter. *Teresa A. Olbrich, 79, Rockford, Ill.*

789   Had a dog named Chelsea whom she loved dearly. *Jolene Blackburn Robison Wahgren, 68, Oceanport, N.J.*

790   Wasn't afraid to try new things. *Patricia Yanni, 78, Geneva, Ill.*

791   Loved Jesus, Elvis, Dr. Pepper and her family. *Myra Janet Headley, 72, Memphis*

792   World War II defense worker. *Jeannette M. Brown, 94, Amesbury, Mass.*

793   Successful business owner in construction and recycling. *Richard M. Cieslak, 76, Red Bud, Ill.*

794   Loved traveling in an R.V. *Irvin Alder, 91, Novi, Mich.*

795   Artist at heart. *Patricia L. Henry, 102, Dearborn, Mich.*

796   Taught math for twenty-five years at Voluntown Elementary School. *Ina Macko, 96, Griswold, Conn.*

797   He loved all animals, music, and community bingo. *Randolph Maitz, 56, Madison, Conn.*

798   Teacher and reading specialist. *Mary Elizabeth Parr, 80, Connecticut*

799   Her family believed she would have stayed with them through the traditional Navajo lifespan of 102 years. *Mary Ann Yazzie, 96, Farmington, N.M.*

800   Epic in every sense of the word. *Richard L. Houle, 86, Bedford, N.H.*

801   Agent who turned on the C.I.A. *Ralph W. McGehee, 92, Falmouth, Maine*

802   Worked in libraries for over twenty years. *Rosemary Ann Hughes, 90, Danbury, Conn.*

803   Made the best baklava ever. *Maria Tassiopoulos, 78, Braintree, Mass.*

804   Worked beside her husband to transform a rundown dairy farm into a flourishing business. *Edna Saikkonen Alve, 92, Spencer, N.Y.*

805   Former mayor, sportscaster. *Raymond Geraci, 91, Highland Park, Ill.*

806   Enjoyed serving as registrar with the D.A.R. *Patricia A. Carrigan, 85, Rush County, Ind.*

807   Her dinners were mouthwateringly good and usually topped off with a homemade pie or cake. *Nancy A. Richard, 83, Marblehead, Mass.*

808   Passionate Boston sports fan. *Edgar Orlando De La Roca, 46, Peabody, Mass.*

809   Faced the challenges of life with a smile and positive attitude. *Clementine E. Jamgochian, 95, Peabody, Mass.*

810   Enjoyed a career in wholesale floorcovering. *Douglas Hanby, 86, Shreveport, La.*

811   "uncannily accurate" in his predictions. *Philip Braverman, 87, East Northport, N.Y.*

812   Vintage Mississippi macho man. *Bennie Webb, 85, Bolingbrook, Ill.*

813   Fierce and vivacious. *Krist Angielen Guzman, 35, Bolingbrook, Ill.*

814   Longtime member of the Sandston Garden Club. *Gertrude Clemmer, 91, Sandston, Va.*

815   Two-time Purple Heart recipient. *Patrick Conran, 91, Riverside, Ill.*

816   Talented painter well known for his landscapes. *Joseph Angeline, 74, Edison, N.J.*

817   Worked for years at many local nursing homes. *John Pope, 53, Haydenville, Mass.*

818   Made his career as a groundbreaking photographic chemist with Polaroid . *Paul James Nagy, 83, Charlottesville, Va.*

819   Longtime AT&T executive. *Frank McClellan Worthington, 84, Morristown, N.J.*

820   Retired head nurse who mastered Persian cooking. *Marjorie P. Tabechian, 86, New York*

821   Retired as the postmaster at the Mingo Post Office. *Jeanette Marie Baldwin, 88, Mingo, Iowa*

822   Quick with his fists in the ring. *Robert William Dietz, 86, Michigan*

823   Talented tennis player. *Muriel E. Lundgren, 91, Haverhill, Mass.*

824   A long career in finance. *Lawrence Littig, 81, Norwalk, Conn.*

825   Collector of people, laughter and good stories. *Bette Jones, 80, Farmington, Conn.*

826   Explored his Scandinavian roots. *Arthur Charles Lindholm, 69, Minnesota*

827   Stockbroker and a great listener. *Edward L. Ghidotti, 87, Upper Arlington, Ohio*

828   Skilled artist, professional wedding cake decorator and quilter. *Mae T. Roser, 92, Manchester, Conn.*

829   A twenty-seven-year career at General Motors. *Shirley Crute, 83, Ossining, N.Y.*

830   Was in charge of The Bethlehem Globe Times's printing department for many years. *John P. Derrico, 78, Fountain Hill, Pa.*

831   Followed her passion in breeding dogs. *Constance M. O'Connor, 76, South Berwick, Maine*

832   Rising phoenix. *Arlene M. Horowitz, 78, Wynnewood, Pa.*

833   Blessed with a coloratura soprano voice and loved to sing "Ave Maria." *Pilar Molina Reyes Rodriques, 89, Plantsville, Conn.*

834   Loved being Grandpa to his "little man" and "sweet pea." *Robert M. Shaw, 69, Beverly, Mass.*

835   Foster mother for over ten years. *Marsha Lee Holiday, 75, North Andover, Mass.*

836   Went to college at forty-five. *Rosemary Hoell Rushka, 89, San Mateo, Calif.*

837   Self-taught musician. *Kenneth A. Rago, 85, Pocasset, Mass.*

838   Survived by her longtime companion and many nieces and nephews. *Rosalie J. Downes Emrich, 97, Catonsville, Md.*

839   World War II veteran, and he proudly drove for generals. *Frank M. Goewey Jr., 95, North Carolina*

840   All-American athlete. *Gomer Richards Jr., 84, West Hurley, N.Y.*

841   Extraordinary photographer, amateur radio operator and gifted musician. *Edward J. Deasy Jr., 71, Charlottesville, Va.*

842   Spent countless hours teaching friends how to water ski. *Harrison Solliday, 85, Des Moines*

843   Town official in Massachusetts. *Robert F. Brady Jr., 65, Avon, Mass.*

844   Loving stay-at-home mom. *Eileen Marie Stanton, 73, Grand Forks, N.D.*

845   Loved all animals. *Cheryl E. Petty, 67, Columbus, Ind.*

846   Proud of her Scottish heritage. *Arlene Muriel MacIntyre, 84, West Hartford, Conn.*

847   Played for the New York Giants as a halfback. *Deane K. Felter, 82, Cromwell, Conn.*

848   Enjoyed crafts, crocheting, playing cards, and board games. *Elaine Jeannette Beaulieu, 90, East Hartford, Conn.*

849   Known for her respect for animals and her love of physical health. *Laura Yopp, 85, South Windsor, Conn.*

850   Raised and trained Labrador retrievers for search and rescue operations. *Robert Woodward, 70, Phenix City, Ala.*

851   Decorated Vietnam War veteran. *Vince Woodward, 77, Columbus, Ga.*

852   Last living woman member of the W.W. II Monuments team. *Motoko Fujishiro Huthwaite, 92, Taylor, Mich.*

853   Onetime publisher of the newspaper The Phoenix. *Michael Armstrong, 79, New York City*

854   Many will miss her infectious, sometimes mischievous laughter. *Durlene Clontz Shuffler, 85, Morganton, N.C.*

855   His passion for learning was insatiable. *Carl Gunther Reiss, 81, Winston-Salem, N.C.*

856   Loved music, especially Christmas carols. *Michael James Reagan, 69, Georgetown, Del.*

857   Retired school counselor. *Loida Cruz Arroyo, 66, Radcliff, Ky.*

858   Had a passion for cars. *Kelly Doyle Oliver, 66, Hastings, Neb.*

859   Talented knitter, a voracious reader, a current events aficionado. *Mary T. King, 94, Dorchester, Mass.*

860   Active in the League of Women Voters. *Mary Doyle Hovanec, 84, Baltimore*

861   Held membership in genealogy societies too numerous to mention. *Anna Elizabeth Pearson Lugg, 90, Hillsborough, N.J.*

862   Housekeeper at Riverside Community Hospital for twenty-five years. *Rosa Luna, 68, California*

863   Remembered for the "nana blankets" she made for her newborn grandchildren. *Anna M. Gayton, 82, Peabody, Mass.*

864   Sheriff's dispatcher. *Nikima Thompson, 41, Broward County, Fla.*

865   Avid skier. *Donald Martin Puffer, 84, Foxboro, Mass.*

866   Navy veteran and the proprietor of Ed's Variety Store in Selkirk. *Edward J. Bridgeford Jr., 90, Albany, N.Y.*

867   Loved to travel and dance. *Maria Lopez, 63, Burbank, Ill.*

868   Taught in the Bridgewater public elementary schools. *Dorothy V. Indeck, 95, Bridgewater, N.J.*

869   Loved being quiet at the beach. *Jeanne Madden Cibroski, 79, Cape Cod, Mass.*

870   Amazing in every sense of the word. *Mary Ellen Houle, 80, Bedford, N.H.*

871   Artist specializing in pastels and sketches. *Geraldine Marie McGovern, 72, Massachusetts*

872   Belonged to several fraternal organizations. *Gerald Alton Cook, 86, New Jersey*

873   Certified horticulturist. *Jean M. Winterbottom, 82, Farmington Hills, Mich.*

874   The presence of Paul Bunyan and the demeanor of a kitten. *William Jonathan Glenney, 73, Vernon, Conn.*

875   Feisty and fun to be with. *Wilma Ruth Montgomery, 91, Phoenix*

876   Served in the Army and worked forty-plus years at Chase Bank. *Guy A. LaVignera, 76, Morganville, N.J.*

877   Engineer always interested in learning new things. *Thomas F. McDermott, 84, Massachusetts*

878   Entered real estate in 1995 as a second career. *Deloris C. Traver, 79, Poughkeepsie, N.Y.*

879   Founded his own company, World Insurance Association, Inc. *Wayne Drye, 78, Atlanta*

880   Always trying to better herself and family. *Hildur T. Stanton, 91, New York*

881   Champion for the rights of Hispanic women. *Juanita Sanchez-Valdez, 90, Glendale, Ariz.*

882   Interior designer blending Sikhism through her life. *Jaimala Singh, 65, Baltimore*

883   Woman of many talents. *Susan C. Menoche, 69, Lincoln, R.I.*

884   Very active in the support of 4-H clubs. *Betty Jo Barney, 91, Green Valley, Ariz.*

885   Well-known for her ready smile. *Linda Benedict, 63, Lakewood, N.J.*

886   Longtime grocery store manager and sports team booster. *James Ronald Conley, 68, Battle Creek, Mich.*

887   Always room at the table for her to feed anyone who showed up. *Grace Lee Hargrave Cradeur, 83, Crowley, La.*

888   If anyone enjoyed the variety life has to offer, he did. *Richard Lynn Heggen, 72, Des Moines*

889   Loved photography, fishing, road trips with friends and time with her family. *Terri Lynn Clark, 60, Des Moines*

890   Authored many stories, articles, and an unpublished novel. *Richard Edward Rutledge, 87, Folsom, Calif.*

891   Gave every bit of herself to her family. *Barbara E. Woznicki, 85, Newington, Conn.*

892   Worked as a school bus driver for thirty years. *Betty Eleanor Fennelly, 87, Cromwell, Conn.*

893   Enjoyed playing euchre with her lifelong girlfriends. *Evelyn Gertrude Brant-Graf, 87, Zionsville, Ind.*

894   Attended every Presidential inauguration from 1965 until 2012. *Alexander Leon Lloyd, 76, Maryland*

895   Fell ill in prison shortly before he was to be released. *Melford Henson, 65, Chino, Calif.*

896   First woman elected to the Pohick vestry. *Anne Turner Gaillard, 76, Mobile, Ala.*

897   Worked for the F.B.I. during World War II. *Grace Nutland, 102, Paramus, N.J.*

898   Owner of the beloved Bread Stuy coffee shop. *Lloyd Cornelius Porter, 49, New York City*

899   Only one in the family unable to get a green card. *Carlos Ernesto Escobar Mejia, 57, San Diego*

900   Known as the "Bookie," she would take and place bets on anything. *Merlene Sue Hughes, 67, South Sioux City, Neb.*

901   Cosmetologist who long survived a brain aneurysm. *Arlene Chesley, 78, La Plata, Md.*

902   Remembered for his successful career as a tango dancer. *Wilman Sanchez Cabrera, 59, New York City*

903   She had that Irish wit. *Florence Cahill Flaherty, 96, Brewster, Mass.*

904   Bob Dylan's No. 1 fan and a lover of nature. *Alexandra Louise Polansky, 62, New Jersey*

905   Truly a free spirit. *Lawrence W. Stedl, 68, Green Bay, Wis.*

906   Co-owner of Johnnies Sandwich Shop. *Dale A. Boston, 81, Massachusetts*

907   Former member of the Quadrille and Colonial Dames of America. *Bettie London Traxler, 97, Greenville, S.C.*

908   Advocate for the Alliance for the Mentally Ill. *Roberta Gulick, 90, Wrentham, Mass.*

909   Avid reader, an accomplished chess player, and an exceptional marksman. *Thomas Kevin Milo Jr., 43, Westchester County, N.Y.*

910   Long-time member of Grace Lutheran Church. *Florence Ethel Buenzly, 99, Allentown, Pa.*

911   Former boxing trainer who owned a well-known Times Square bar. *Jimmy Glenn, 89, Manhattan, N.Y.*

912   Found joy in every aspect of her life. *Amelia Scott Dougherty, 84, Media, Pa.*

913   Never far from his motorcycles or hot rods. *Billy Ostland, 64, Delaware County, Pa.*

914   Seamstress who worked at several sewing mills. *Joan A. Lenhart, 84, Wyomissing, Pa.*

915   Involved with the development of Air Force technologies. *Douglas*

H. Diamond, 82, Chelmsford, Mass.

916 **Man of few words.** *Claude Reno Doucette, 84, Connecticut*

917 **Member of the Old Coots on Scoots motorcycle club.** *John F. Von Sternberg Jr., 79, Mountain Lakes, N.J.*

918 **Served as a deacon and especially enjoyed a mission trip to Peru.** *James C. Whittemore, 83, Johnson City, N.Y.*

919 **Served with the Army National Guard for twenty years.** *Frankie L. Morris Sr., 64, Wooster, Ohio*

920 **Enjoyed her daily coffee with her mother-in-law.** *Cindy Lou Mack, 62, Waverly, N.Y.*

921 **One half of Siegfried & Roy.** *Roy Horn, 75, Las Vegas*

922 **Was married for fifty-nine years.** *Lucy Yanushefski, 95, West Chester, Pa.*

923 **Had a passion for cooking, fishing, skiing, and cars.** *Walter Everett Barton, 67, Poughkeepsie, N.Y.*

924 **Served on the Pulaski Polka Days Committee for many years.** *Randy Wichlacz, 62, Pulaski, Wis.*

925 **Cherished mother.** *Alice Glazer, 79, Silver Spring, Md.*

926 **He trained aboard the first nuclear-powered vessel in the U.S. fleet.** *Donald Geoffrey Helliwell, 86, Westfield, Mass.*

927 **Very active in the Portuguese community.** *Peter S. Miguel Jr., 66, Nashua, N.H.*

928 **Served as the Iowa president of the League of Women Voters.** *Janice L. McNelly, 79, Iowa*

929 **Nothing brought him greater joy than taking his boys on hikes.** *Robert Grant Conner, 96, Easthampton, Mass.*

930 **Lifelong resident of Parsippany, where he was a friend to everyone.** *Leon Martin Beels, 69, Morristown, N.J.*

931 **Loved painting, crocheting and spending time with her family.** *Tracie L. Heverly, 58, Sebring, Ohio*

932 **Held many jobs throughout the years.** *Wilfred Jay Sikkema, 81, Clinton, Iowa*

933 **Long-term school district employee.** *Michael Angelo Church, 72, Plainfield, N.J.*

934 **Graduate of Gloucester City High School class of 2009.** *Rocco Anthony Ward Jr., 29, Gloucester City, N.J.*

935 **Lifelong resident of Westernport.** *Tonna Lee Pratt, 69, Westernport, Md.*

936 **We will forever remember her saying, "Keep the water in the pool!"** *Elizabeth N. Updegrave, 91, Reading, Pa.*

937 **Performed in many productions at the Salt City Playhouse.** *Elaine Menchel Marcus, 75, Syracuse, N.Y.*

938 **Lifelong career in health care.** *Katherine Ann Birkmaier, 64, Bridgeport, Conn.*

939 **Admired for her fashion sense, especially her collection of hats.** *Mattie F. Adams, 89, Niagara Falls, N.Y.*

940 **World War II veteran.** *Nelson Henry Jr., 96, Philadelphia*

941 **An esoteric sense of humor.** *P. Michael Baillargeon, 75, Massachusetts*

942 **Loved to spend time at the beach soaking in the sun.** *Ellen Marie Pauze, 94, Londonderry, N.H.*

943 **Died after being released from ICE detention.** *Oscar López Acosta, 42, Morrow County, Ohio*

944 **Had a passion for decorating and an artistic streak.** *Margaret MacVeagh Schweers, 93, New Jersey*

945 **Enjoyed delivering day-old bread to church, family and friends.** *Raymond Gayle Burgett, 86, Des Moines*

946 **Kind and brave man, never forgetful of his roots.** *James Ventrillo, 77, Methuen, Mass.*

947 **Lifetime resident of Easton.** *Carl A. Philipp, 84, Easton, Pa.*

948 **Enjoyed golf and watching the Hawkeyes.** *Mary A. Cole, 93, Cedar Rapids, Iowa*

949 **Veteran of the Vietnam War.** *Randolph Warren Whipple, 78, Plainville, Conn.*

950 **Korean War hero and inventor.** *Francis A. Kennedy, 95, Clarence, N.Y.*

951 **Mother to a generation of AIDS patients.** *Nita Pippins, 93, Manhattan, N.Y.*

952 **Lifelong Phillies and Eagles fan.** *Michael J. Mchugh, 88, Philadelphia*

953 **Liked golfing and sewing, but loved spending time with family and friends.** *Mary Ann Bregar, 91, Ohio*

954 **Many will remember her half-moon cookies.** *Jeanette Gilmour, 86, Marcellus, N.Y.*

955 **True renaissance man.** *Steven P. St. Laurent, 67, East Syracuse, N.Y.*

956 **Hauled milk by the can, and later with a bulk milk truck.** *Howard J. Bender, 88, Lancaster, Wis.*

957 **Managed Answer Iowa Answering Service in Waterloo for many years.** *JoAnne Katherine Walther, 74, Cedar Falls, Iowa*

958 **Loved going to the zoo, watching soap operas and window shopping.** *Marilyn Luella Tayse, 75, Ohio*

959 **Made each of her children and grandchildren a quilt.** *Londia Viola Mongold Deavers, 88, Harrisonburg, Va.*

960 **Sunday school teacher.** *Mildred W. Blough, 92, Wooster, Ohio*

961 **Priest who sought "to help people to be happy and holy."** *Roland Henry Lacasse, 88, Massachusetts*

962 **Avid St. Louis Cardinals and Minnesota Vikings fan.** *Danny Ray Bierman, 61, Muscatine, Iowa*

963 **Painted Hudson River landscapes, portraits and still lifes.** *Marguerite Peyser, 71, New York City*

964 **Enjoyed trying her luck in the casino.** *Irene S. Allen, 93, Ambler, Pa.*

965 **Loved dogs, puzzles and books.** *Darla Eileen Brown, 54, Sioux City, Iowa*

966 **Voracious reader.** *Margueritte Martha McCain, 96, Tulsa, Okla.*

967 **Avid member of the Antique Automobile Club of America.** *Betty M. Bradshaw, 87, Charlottesville, Va.*

968 **Sixty-seven-year member of Pipefitters Local 636.** *Ronald R. Erdman, 90, Novi, Mich.*

969 **Her famous quote was "I am as good as you are, as bad as I am."** *Nancy Taylor, 85, Tinton Falls, N.J.*

970 **Loved being a mom.** *Mary Santiago, 44, Evanston, Ill.*

971 **Pioneer in the field of autism research.** *Thomas A. Williams, 62, Ohio*

972 **Enjoyed visiting casinos, playing bingo and scratching lottery tickets.** *Carmen Rodriguez, 85, Windsor Locks, Conn.*

973 **Attended electronics schools in the Navy.** *Russell D. Green, 92, Crawfordsville, Ind.*

974 **Proud Army veteran who served during WWII.** *Duane G. Vock, 92, Mission, Kan.*

975 **Emigrated to the United States in 1963 as a medical resident.** *Pio Mactal Vilar Jr., 81, Summerlin, Nev.*

976 **Twenty-eight-year veteran of the United States Army.** *Alan Michael Twofoot, 51, Nashua, N.H.*

977 **Engine technician in the New Hampshire Air National Guard.** *Carl J. Hebert Sr., 76, Manchester, N.H.*

978 **Had a passion for golf and bridge.** *Joyce Roberts, 96, Portland, Maine*

979 **Proud member of the Ancient Order of Hibernians.** *Robert M. Sullivan, 88, Springfield, Pa.*

980 **Retired from Verizon after over forty years of service.** *Timothy E. Murray, 82, Ocean View, Del.*

981 **Survived the German invasion and occupation of Poland during World War II.** *Genowefa Kochanek, 98, Massachusetts*

982 **An Iowa Air National Guardsman.** *Patrick C. Parks, 85, Sergeant Bluff, Iowa*

983 **Attended the Illinois College of Optometry.** *Russell Arnold Nielsen, 96, Cedar Falls, Iowa*

984 **Employed at General Electric for thirty-eight years.** *Richard C. Schug, 83, Syracuse, N.Y.*

985 **Filled her life by caring for her children and grandchildren.** *Diana G. DeVito Swist, 80, Norwalk, Conn.*

986 **Favorite of all her nieces and nephews.** *Janice Lin Bisley, 70, Bristol, Conn.*

987 **A long, successful retail career, primarily at Macy's.** *Joel I. Sneider, 74, Miami Beach*

988 **Navajo teacher with a sense of duty.** *Marie Pino, 67, Albuquerque*

989 **Happiest when she was barefoot in her flower garden.** *Jean D. Tobin, 91, Bucks County, Pa.*

990 **Her last words were "thank you."** *Cornelia Ann Hunt, 87, Virginia Beach*

991 **Will be missed at Mad Jack Brewing.** *Dennis Alan Bradt, 29, Colonie, N.Y.*

992 **Never missed "Wheel of Fortune," "Jeopardy" or "Lawrence Welk."** *Rita Paas, 88, Comstock Park, Mich.*

993 **A lifelong career with WHIL radio.** *David F. Savitt, 86, Ludlow, Mass.*

994 **Served with the U.S. Marines during the Vietnam War.** *Paul A. Hamel, 80, Westminster, Mass.*

995 **Her authentic Greek cooking and dancing was second to none.** *Dorothy Spanos, 90, Orangeburg, N.Y.*

996 **Sketched advertisements for large department stores.** *Frances A. Orsini, 91, Brick, N.J.*

997 **Social worker and political fundraiser.** *Dolores M. DeLaurentis, 89, Bethlehem, Pa.*

998 **Owned a local bar.** *William Hrabnicky, 76, Cleveland*

999 **Lived in many places as an Army wife before settling in New Jersey.** *Dolores M. Madera, 91, Oceanport, N.J.*

1000 **Champion of people with speech disorders.** *Annie Glenn, 100, St. Paul, Minn.*